Act It Out

Books by Bernice Wells Carlson

DO IT YOURSELF!

MAKE IT YOURSELF!

JUNIOR PARTY BOOK

FUN FOR ONE—OR TWO

ACT IT OUT

MAKE IT AND USE IT

THE RIGHT PLAY FOR YOU

LISTEN! AND HELP TELL THE STORY

LET'S PRETEND IT HAPPENED TO YOU

PLAY A PART

FUNNY-BONE DRAMATICS

BERNICE WELLS CARLSON

Act It Out

ILLUSTRATED BY LASZLO MATULAY

Abingdon Press

NASHVILLE

ISBN 0-687-00713-5 *(cloth)*
ISBN 0-687-00714-3 *(paper)*

I WOULD LIKE TO THANK the many people who helped me prepare this book: Miss E. Ann Brush, Puppet Class Instructor, Y.W.C.A., New Brunswick, New Jersey; Miss Iris Vinton, Director, Publications Service, Boys' Clubs of America; Mrs. Joseph Vertrees and her Brownies in Troop 125, Middlebush, New Jersey; Mr. Anthony Zydycryn, Boy Scout leader, Richmond, California; members of Cub Pack No. 7, Middlebush, New Jersey; my husband, Dr. C. W. Carlson; my children, Christine and Philip; and their many cousins and friends.

THE AUTHOR

TO HELEN AND BUD

Contents

Act It Out

ACTING IS FUN! You are acting when you pretend you are a cowboy or a queen, when you play a dramatic game, or when you take part in a program. You can put on a performance alone — a "one-man show" — or you can be part of a team in a dramatic stunt. You can be in front of the audience in a play or behind the scene for a puppet show. There are many kinds of acting.

Start with something easy. Play a game in which you disguise your voice and imitate someone's actions. Get together with your friends and make up a story to act out. Pretend you are characters from some other world or from ages past. Imitate actors on radio or television programs, in movies, or stage plays. Write a play. Join with your friends to act it out. Or act out some story you know well.

As your interest in acting grows and your skill improves, put on more polished play productions.

Acting with puppets is fun too. Make simple puppets. Tell a story, wiggling each puppet as it speaks, changing your voice for each character. Then make other kinds of puppets and work out a play to show your family and your neighbors.

ACT IT OUT is a starting book. It suggests games, plays, stunts, pageants, tableaux, and pantomimes. It tells how to make and use puppets and marionettes.

Use your own ideas! Do not hesitate to change the plays in this book. Solve your stage problems by using your imagination and by persuading the audience to use theirs.

No matter what kind of acting you choose — simple or complicated, real characters or puppets — have fun when you *act it out!*

I. You're the Actor

ACTING is for everyone. It is for the person who naturally likes to entertain a group; it is also for the person who is shy and awkward — or who thinks he is. The chances are he hasn't had an opportunity to do simple acting.

Several kinds of acting are suggested in this section. Choose the kind you like best. You can start with a game, a group stunt, or a tableau in which anyone can take part. Or, if you have already had some experience in acting, you can put on a pantomime or a play. Encourage your friends to become actors too. It is a good way to have fun together.

Acting Games

WHEN YOU PLAY these games, you are acting, even though you have no lines to learn and no story to tell. You may change your voice, use motions, or in some other way show that you are someone other than yourself.

POOR PUSSY

One player is Pussy. All the other players sit in a circle around him. Pussy kneels before one player and says, *Meow, meow, meow,* in the funniest way he can. He may make any kind of face or he may make motions with his front paws, but he must not touch the player before whom he is kneeling.

The player strokes Pussy's head three times and says, "Poor Pussy, poor Pussy, poor Pussy." He tries to keep a perfectly straight face. If he laughs or smiles, he becomes Pussy.

If Pussy cannot make the first player laugh or smile, he goes to the next player. If Pussy cannot make anyone in the circle laugh or smile, he must pay a forfeit, and another player becomes Pussy.

If there are many players, divide into groups of five or six.

STATUES

One player is IT. Before each game he says, "I am going to choose the prettiest statue." Or he may say, "I am going to choose the funniest statue." Then he whirls each player and lets him go.

The player lands in some unusual position. He stays in that position as still as a statue. When all the players are statues, IT looks carefully at each one and then chooses the prettiest or the funniest.

The chosen statue becomes IT.

BLIND MAN'S FARM

Before the game starts, an area is marked off for the barnyard. No player may leave the barnyard. One player is the farmer; the other players are animals.

The farmer is blindfolded and turned around three times. While he counts to ten, the animals scatter within the barnyard.

The farmer gropes his way around until he finds a player. "I have found you, little animal. Who are you?" asks the farmer.

The player who was caught makes a noise like an animal: *bow-wow, moo-moo, baa-baa,* or even *owww,* like a stray coyote or wolf. The blind farmer tries to guess the player. If he guesses correctly, the player becomes the farmer. If the farmer guesses incorrectly, the game is repeated. If the farmer cannot guess correctly after trying three times, another player becomes the farmer.

WHO KNOCKS?

IT is seated in a chair with his eyes shut and his head in his hands. The other players stand behind him. One of them steps forward and touches IT on his shoulder.

15

"Who knocks?" asks IT.

"It is I, the ogre." (or some other storybook character), says the player who tapped, disguising his voice to make it sound like an ogre. Or he may say, "It is I, the elf," or whatever character he chooses to be.

If IT guesses the player correctly, that player becomes IT. If IT guesses incorrectly, IT must close his eyes again while someone else taps. If IT cannot guess who tapped after three players have tried, he chooses another player to be IT.

MERRY CHRISTMAS!

Players sit in a straight line. IT stands in front of one player. This player asks IT, "What would you like for Christmas?"

"Can you guess?" answers IT. He then makes some motion that will describe what he wants for Christmas. He may pretend to blow a horn, pat a kitten or puppy, or kick a football.

If the player guesses correctly, IT says, "Merry Christmas!" and the player becomes IT. If the player guesses incorrectly, IT stands in front of another player.

You can say, "Happy Easter!" "Happy birthday!" or whatever happens to be appropriate when you play this game.

16

SANTA'S TOYS

Ten or more players sit in a circle. Each player is given the name of a toy — a doll, horn, drum, car, etc. There should be more than one of each kind of toy.

IT stands in the center of the circle and starts to tell a story about the toys. The story should be very simple and should include all the toys. For example, IT might begin: "It was Christmas Eve. Santa had a big smile on his face when he looked at all the *dolls,* the *horns,* the *drums,* and the *cars.* I am certainly proud of my *toys —* "

When IT says *doll,* all the dolls stand up, bow at the waist, and say "Mama." When IT says *horn,* all the horns stand up, pretend to blow, and go *toot-toot.* When IT says *drum,* all the drums stand up, pretend to beat a drum, and say *rub-a-dub.* When IT says *car,* all the cars stand up, pretend to drive, and say *honk-honk.*

When IT says *toys,* all the toys change chairs. IT tries to slip into an empty chair. The player who is left standing becomes IT. The first IT takes the name of a toy and the game continues.

You can tell many other stories to make this game appropriate at any time of year. Players can be *witches, cats,* and *ghosts,* and change chairs on the word *Halloween.* They can be *rabbits, ducks,* and *hens,* and change chairs on the words *Easter eggs.* They can be *horses, Indians,* and *bandits,* and change chairs on the word *stagecoach.*

17

WORD CHARADES

There are a number of ways to play charades. The important thing is to set down one set of rules and stick to them.

The players are divided into groups. Each group goes by itself and chooses a word of more than one syllable to act out.

When the players get together again, the leader of the first group indicates with his fingers the number of syllables in the chosen word. The players put on a short dialogue for each syllable and one in which they use the whole word. Other players try to guess the word after the last dialogue has been presented.

For example. The word is *handkerchief.* The leader raises three fingers. The dialogue goes:

First dialogue. First Player (*going to second*). I'd like to shake the *hand* of the man who made that speech.

Second Player. Thank you, sir.

Second dialogue. First Player. Look at the dog I found.

Second Player. I never saw such a homely *cur.*

Third dialogue. (*Players are seated in a pow-wow circle, pretending to beat drums.*) First Player. Now is the time of the festival of the moon.

Second Player. Yes. It is time for the *chief* to speak.

Fourth dialogue. First Player. Let's see if you're ready for school. Your hair's combed. You have your rubbers, your *handkerchief,* and your books. Good-by.

Second Player. Good-by.

Pantomime Games

WHEN YOU pantomime, you act without using words. You don't move your lips. But the expression on your face and your gestures tell what you are doing.

Before you begin, try to think of every motion you will use. Don't hurry your actions. Most beginners perform too fast.

These games will test your ability to act.

WHAT AM I DOING?

Choose something that you would like to do. See if you can go through the motions so well that someone else can guess what you are doing. Finish your act before he guesses.

Here are some situations you might pantomime: baking a cake, playing hopscotch, riding on a bus or train, buying something at a department store, watching a ball game, or eating peanuts.

HERE WE COME!

This game is played in a large place, such as a gymnasium or field. There is a center line, and a goal line for each team.

Players are divided into two teams. The first team goes behind its goal line and thinks of some action it will pantomime, like washing windows, playing baseball, or selling hats.

Both teams come to within three feet of the center line. Each team stands in a line. They say:

First Team. Here we come!

Second Team. Where from?

First Team. New York.

Second Team. What's your trade?

First Team. Lemonade.

Second Team. What are your initials?

First Team. W. W. (for *washing windows,* or the first letters of the words that they will pantomime).

Second Team. Get to work and show us some.

The first team pantomimes its actions. Any member of the second team may call out the answer when he thinks he has it. If his guess is correct, the first team runs back to its goal. Members of the second team chase them and tag as many as they can. Everyone tagged goes over to the other team.

Then the second team chooses a pantomime and the first team guesses.

PASS IT ALONG

Players stand in a line. The first player pretends to pick up something and pass it to the player next to him. He will pick up different things in different ways. A big stone will be hard to lift. He will strain his back. He will grab the stone with both hands, fingers outstretched. For a pin, he will use his thumb and first finger. He will hold a baby in his arms and pass it gently.

The second player tries to pass the object in the same way that the first player did. When the last player receives the object, he tries to guess what he has. If he guesses wrong, each player up the line has a chance to guess. If no one can guess, the first player tells. Then he goes to the end of the line and the game begins again.

If there are a large number of players, divide into teams. One person tells the leader of each team what object he must pick up. See which team can guess what is passed down the line.

PANTOMIME PARTNERS

Make a list of actions to pantomime — patting a kitty, throwing a baseball, fixing a car. Have half as many subjects as players.

Give each player a slip of paper with the subject he is to pantomime written on it. The subject should be kept secret.

At a signal all players start to pantomime. They must watch the other players at the same time. Each player tries to pick out the other player who is doing the same pantomime he is. The first pair to get together wins, but the game continues until all players are matched.

WHO AM I?

Choose a type of person to represent. Pantomime his entrance into a room. If you are a baby, creep. If you are an old man, bend a little and walk slowly. How would a nine-year-old boy enter? See if other players can guess who you are.

Take turns doing different things the way different people would do them. Sit down, eat, greet someone, etc. See if other players can guess who you are.

GUESS THESE NURSERY RHYMES

See if you can pantomime the actions of a character in a nursery rhyme so well that other players can guess who you are. Finish your act before the guessing begins.

Form teams of two or three actors. Each team chooses a rhyme and pantomimes the actions described in it. The other teams try to guess the rhyme.

TITLE CHARADES

Title charades are pantomimed. The group is divided into two teams. Each team goes by itself and chooses titles for the other team to act out. These titles may be in different categories: nursery rhymes, songs, books, or movies. The titles, one for each member of the opposing team, are written on separate slips of paper.

When both teams are ready, they come to the center of the room and face each other. Each team puts its slips face down in a pile.

A member of the first team draws a title from the pile of the second team. He tells his team the category. He may say, "It is a nursery

rhyme." From then on he must use only signals and pantomime.

The first signal is always the number of words in the title. This is indicated by holding up the correct number of fingers. The next signal shows which word the player will pantomime first. He may wish to pantomime the most important word rather than the first word.

To signal for a "little" word (an article, preposition, or conjunction) the player crosses his index fingers near their tips.

Suppose the title is "The Three Little Pigs." The player says, "This is a nursery story." He holds up four fingers for the number of words. Next he holds up one finger for the first word, then crosses his index fingers near their tips to show that this first word is a "little" word.

Sometimes when a player cannot act out a word, he holds his hand to his ear. That means he is going to indicate a word which rhymes with the word. Instead of trying to act like a *pig,* the player may hold his hand to his ear and then stretch his arms far apart to indicate *big.*

Teams take turns guessing.

GRAB-BAG PANTOMIMES

Put a number of articles into a paper bag — one thing for each player. You can use anything that is not sharp: a pencil, a powder puff, a fancy handkerchief, a clothespin, a spool of thread, an eraser, an empty chewing-gum wrapper, a stick, a paintbrush.

Pass the bag to each player. Ask him to close his eyes and then pull out one article. This is his property, or "prop," for a pantomime.

Each player pantomimes a short scene, using the prop he drew. When he has finished, the other players try to guess what he was doing.

TRADES

One player is King. All the other players choose trades. Each names his trade and shows how to do it. The carpenter pounds, the mason lays bricks, the farmer milks cows, the housewife sweeps, the baker kneads bread, the truck driver steers his truck, and so on. The King chooses a trade, too. He might dig ditches or plant a garden.

At the start of the game everyone goes through the motions of his

trade. Suddenly the King stops doing his trade and begins to do some-one else's trade. For example, he might pound like the carpenter.

Everyone except the carpenter stops work. King and carpenter work together for a few seconds. Then the King goes back to his own trade and everyone starts his work again.

A player is out of the game if he does not stop work when the King picks up a new trade, or if he does stop work if the King chooses his trade, or if he fails to start work when the King resumes his own trade. The game is most fun if the King changes trades often.

After the King has put two players out of the game, he chooses a new player to be King, and the game starts again.

Pantomime Plays

When you can pantomime well, you are ready to present pantomime plays. You can make up scenes of your own. Or you can pantomime old ballads and stories. Choose the ones which have plenty of action.

When acting out an old fantastic story, exaggerate your actions. If you are a hero or heroine, swing your arms in big gestures. If you are a villain, glower and stamp your feet. If you must faint, flop. When doing a realistic pantomime, make every motion and every facial expression just as you would make it if you were the person in the play.

Sometimes your actions will tell the entire story. At other times, a reader or chorus tells the story while you act it out.

EXCURSIONS

Think of some place to go. Imagine what you would do if you were there. See if you can pantomime so well that other people can follow the story. Act out the following scenes, then think of some of your own.

The Big Catch. Dig the worms. Put down the shovel. Pick up the can and the fishing pole. Walk along happily. Stop at a good spot. Sit

down. Put down the can. Bait the hook. Put the line into the water. Get a few nibbles. Be disappointed. Try again. Catch a little fish. Be disgusted. Throw your line out again. Fall half-asleep, with the pole between your legs. Get a big bite. Wake up suddenly. Catch a big fish.

Rained Out. Find a good spot for a family picnic. Put down the baskets. Throw away stones and sticks that are in the way. Spread the cloth. Start to put food on it. Chase away the flies. Chase away a big dog. Enjoy a few bites of food. Feel a few drops of rain. Start to pick up food just as a big cloudburst comes.

Movie Nuisance. Try to push ahead of someone in line at ticket window. Get shoved back. Impatiently wait your turn. Buy ticket. Drop change. Pick it up. Give ticket to doorman. Buy popcorn. Spill some. Look at it. Give it a kick. Walk down aisle. Spot seat in middle of theater. Crawl over people in row before they have chance to stand. Plop down in seat. Squirm around, getting comfortable. Get interested in movie. Bounce up and down. Get mad when person behind you asks you to sit still. Eat popcorn, spilling it. Watch movie. Laugh, cry, get excited. When movie is over, drop things, take a long time to reach aisle.

SOLDIER, SOLDIER
Characters

SOLDIER   CHORUS

MAIDEN

The CHORUS *stands in a row and either sings or recites the lines of the ballad.* MAIDEN *and* SOLDIER *pantomime in front of* CHORUS.

> Soldier, soldier, won't you marry me
> With musket, fife, and drum?

(*When the* MAIDEN *begs the* SOLDIER *to marry her, she puts out both her arms, pleading with him.*)

> Oh, no, fair maid, I cannot marry you
> For I've got no hat to put on.

(*The* SOLDIER *stands with crossed arms, sternly shaking his head. He makes big sweeping gestures when he points to his hat, and later to other garments which he lacks.*)

> Off she went to her grandfather's chest.
> She got him a hat, the very, very best.
> And the soldier put it on.
> The soldier put it on.

(*Each time the* MAIDEN *goes to her grandfather's chest, she climbs the steps wearily, lifts the heavy lid of the chest, and tenderly takes out the garment. She returns quickly and happily to the* SOLDIER, *proudly giving him the garment. He puts it on with great delight, very pleased with himself.*)

> Soldier, soldier, won't you marry me
> With musket, fife, and drum?
> Oh, no, fair maid, I cannot marry you
> For I've got no coat to put on.
> Off she went to her grandfather's chest.
> She got him a coat, the very, very best.
> And the soldier put it on.
> The soldier put it on.

Soldier, soldier, won't you marry me
With musket, fife, and drum?
Oh, no, fair maid, I cannot marry you
For I've got no shoes to put on.
Off she went to her grandfather's chest.
She got him some shoes, the very, very best.
And the soldier put them on.
The soldier put them on.

Soldier, soldier, won't you marry me
With musket, fife, and drum?
Oh, no, fair maid, I cannot marry you
For I've got no gloves to put on.
Off she went to her grandfather's chest.
She got him some gloves, the very, very best.
And the soldier put them on.
The soldier put them on.

Soldier, soldier, won't you marry me
With musket, fife, and drum?
Oh, no, fair maid, I cannot marry you.
For I have a wife and baby at home.

(*When the* Chorus *sings the last line, the* Maiden *swoons into the arms of the* Chorus. *The* Soldier *admires all the fine new clothes he is wearing, smiles, pleased with himself, waves to the fainting* Maiden, *and walks away.*)

FABLES

Some old familiar fables are easy to pantomime. Plan your motions so that the audience can follow the story. If you wish, pin names on characters to identify them.

Bell the Cat. Cat sleeps in a corner. Mice creep in slowly and view Cat. Leader Mouse points to Cat and then to bell he, Leader Mouse, is holding. (He can pretend to have a bell or use a paper one.) Leader Mouse points again to Cat and to Cat's tail. Mice agree. Then they point to Leader Mouse, indicating that he should tie the bell on the Cat's tail. He shakes his head and points to other Mice, one by one. Each in turn shakes his head and points to Leader Mouse. He stoutly refuses. Cat opens one eye slowly. Then the other eye. Mice draw back in fear. Cat moves his shoulders forward, just a little. Leader Mouse throws down the bell. Mice scramble away. Cat smiles, amused, and goes back to sleep.

The Tortoise and the Hare. Tortoise and Hare meet. Hare thumps his chest, bragging. He motions how fast he can run. Tortoise turns up his nose, shrugs his shoulders, unimpressed. He indicates that he can get to a tree before Hare can. Hare laughs hard. He motions to Fox to come to start race. Fox points to tree to which they will run. Hare and Tortoise agree. Fox lifts three fingers, one at a time, as if counting "one, two, three," then thrusts arm down for "go." HARE takes one or two jumps, stops, and looks back at TORTOISE, who is coming very slowly. HARE sits down and falls asleep. TORTOISE passes HARE. HARE wakes up just as TORTOISE reaches tree. Fox lifts up arm of TORTOISE to indicate the winner. HARE stamps his foot angrily.

ANDROCLES AND THE LION
Characters

LION	SPECTATORS
ANDROCLES	EMPEROR
SOLDIER	

SCENE I, *Jungle.* LION lies panting, as if in great pain. He frequently looks at his paw. ANDROCLES approaches, starts back, looks at LION again, and studies him more carefully. Slowly approaches LION. LION holds out paw, pants in pain. ANDROCLES sees thorn in paw. Cautiously gets near LION. LION looks at him pleadingly. ANDROCLES pulls thorn from paw. LION nods head as if trying to thank ANDROCLES. ANDROCLES pats LION's head and goes away smiling.

SCENE II, *Colosseum in Rome.* SPECTATORS sit at back of stage. EMPEROR is in center. SPECTATORS are laughing. SOLDIER leads in ANDROCLES as a slave. SOLDIER gives ANDROCLES a shove, making him fall on his knees. SPECTATORS laugh and clap. ANDROCLES stands firm, helpless, but not showing his fear. Lion approaches slowly, eyeing Androcles. Suddenly Lion stops. Instead of tearing Androcles to pieces, he rubs against his legs. Androcles recognizes his old friend of the jungle. With his arm around Lion, Androcles faces Emperor. Emperor lifts hand, indicating "Speak." Androcles lifts Lion's paw to show how he pulled out thorn. Emperor puts "thumbs up." Androcles and Lion leave together, both free. Spectators cheer.

REMEMBER THESE?

Pantomime well-known scenes from history. When you have finished a scene, see if your audience can guess who the characters are. You can use props, or you can imagine that you have them.

Ponce de León Looks for Fountain of Youth. Ponce de León and Soldiers come to pool. Ponce de León kneels. Makes cup of hands. Dips them into pool. Lifts hands to drink. Rises. Calls for mirror. Soldier hands mirror to Ponce de León. He looks at himself and shakes his head sadly.

Franklin Discovers Electricity. Franklin enters, carrying kite under his arm. He pulls up his coat collar with his other hand. Slams his hat tighter on his head, indicating that it is cold and windy. Releases kite, and slowly unwinds the string. Looks at key at end of string. Gets a shock. Shows pain. Then smiles.

Washington Throws Coin Across River. Young GEORGE WASHINGTON and FRIEND enter and start to fish. They put down their poles. WASHINGTON takes coin from his pocket. Pretends to throw it across place where he has been fishing. He and FRIEND look happy as they see coin land on opposite bank.

SHADOW PANTOMIMES

Hang a sheet across an opening in front of the place where the actors will perform. This may be across a large doorway or between the partially drawn curtains on a stage. Place lights a short distance behind the sheet. Experiment to find the best position for them.

Actors must stand close to the sheet with their bodies turned so that they cast a profile shadow. They must stand apart or one shadow will block out another. The blocking-out has advantages as well as disadvantages. When a hero thrusts his cardboard sword back of a monster, the shadow looks as if the sword is piercing the beast. Make cardboard properties. These, too, must be shown in profile.

You can pantomime nursery rhymes, scenes from history, episodes from books, or original stories. A reader may tell the story as you act it out. Or you can let the audience guess who the characters are.

Robin Hood Meets Little John. ROBIN HOOD and LITTLE JOHN approach from opposite sides of the stage. They pause a few feet apart. Each motions for the other to stand aside. They meet in the center of the screen and fight with staffs. ROBIN HOOD tumbles over. LITTLE JOHN gives him a hand and helps him up. They shake hands.

King Arthur and the Sword Excalibur. A cardboard sword is stuck into a large carton, representing a rock, center stage. MERLIN enters from one side. ENGLISH NOBLES enter from other side. ARTHUR is last to enter. MERLIN holds crown in one hand. He pantomimes drawing sword from rock, then points to crown. One by one the nobles try to pull out the sword. None can do it. At last ARTHUR steps forward. He pulls out the sword easily. MERLIN holds up crown. ARTHUR kneels before MERLIN, who crowns him king.

THESEUS AND THE MINOTAUR
Characters

READER	MINOTAUR, a monster with head
THESEUS, son of King of Athens	of bull, body of man
ARIADNE, daughter of King of Crete	

READER *reads story as characters shadow-pantomime the action. A sword and a ball of string are the only properties needed.*

Many years ago, the beautiful city of Athens, Greece, was conquered by King Minos of Crete. As a penalty, King Minos required the city to send its seven most noble youths and its seven most beautiful maidens to Crete each year. There they were devoured by a monster, the Minotaur. Among those who went to Crete was Theseus, son of King Aegeus of Athens. (THESEUS *appears. Turn off lights. He exits.*)

Now King Minos of Crete had a beautiful daughter Ariadne. She saw Theseus paraded through the streets at the head of the procession of Athenian youths and maidens. She knew that she must do something to save him. (ARIADNE *appears. Keep lights on.*) Secretly Ariadne ran to the mouth of the Minotaur's cave. There she waited for Theseus to arrive. (ARIADNE *runs to side of stage.*)

When Theseus entered the cave, Ariadne called, "Wait!" (THESEUS *crosses in front of her almost to center stage. She holds up hand. He turns.*)

"Who are you?" asked Theseus. "I did not see you as I passed."

"I am Ariadne, daughter of King Minos. I have come to help you."

"Help me fight the Minotaur? How?" asked Theseus.

"*Shh,*" she cautioned. "Here is a sword. (*Hands* THESEUS *sword.*) And here is a ball of silken thread." (*She holds up ball of string.*)

"Thread?"

"Yes, thread. This cave is a labyrinth. It is filled with many passages. The Minotaur cannot find his way out. Neither can you unless you fasten one end of this thread to the mouth of the cave. Unwind the ball as you walk. After you have killed the Minotaur, follow the thread back to the mouth of the cave."

"Thank you, fair maiden. (*He takes ball of string.*) When I have killed the Minotaur, I shall return to you."

"I shall wait." (*She waves and goes backstage.*)

Theseus fastened the thread to the cave door. (*Goes to wing and hands someone the end of the string. Returns to stage.*) Holding his sword in readiness, he advanced down the long corridor of the cave. Slowly he unwound the thread. (THESEUS *advances. String is kept taut near screen. People off stage on each side hold the string, as* THESEUS *goes back and forth, ending at the point where he started.*)

Cautiously he advanced through the dimly lighted passage. The air was dank. The smell was foul. Yet Theseus pressed forward. On and on he went, sometimes stumbling, sometimes bumping into the darkened jutting rocks. He pushed forward, going farther and farther into the unknown labyrinth, always unwinding his thread carefully. Always he was ready to meet the Minotaur. (*The length of this passage will depend on the width of your screen. If you see that* THESEUS *has traveled far enough,* READER *can leave out a sentence or two.*)

Suddenly Theseus heard a terrible cry. (*Bellow off stage.*) He turned. (*He turns, sword raised.*) No man ever cried like that. No known beast. It was the Minotaur! But Theseus was ready to meet it.

In charged the beast, half man, half bull. (MINOTAUR *charges in. Halts.*) For a moment it paused. In that moment, Theseus struck.

(THESEUS *strikes.*) The Minotaur fell to its knees. (MINOTAUR *falls.*) It rose again to charge. (*Charges.* THESEUS *backs up a little.*) Theseus retreated a few steps, then struck again, and again. (*He strikes again and again.*) The wounded Minotaur fought on. But at last it fell. (MINOTAUR *falls.*) Theseus was upon it. Blow after blow he struck. (*Keeps striking.*) At last the Minotaur was dead. (MINOTAUR *collapses.* THESEUS *poses triumphant above it.*)

Theseus picked up the thread and followed it. (*Begins to wind up string and follow it.*) His heart was light. He had killed the Minotaur. He soon neared the mouth of the cave. There, standing in the entrance, was Ariadne. (*On his last lap back,* ARIADNE *runs to meet him at about center stage.*) She ran to meet him. Together they fled.

Never again did Athens send her youths and maidens to Crete to be devoured by a monster.

Dramatic Stunts

DRAMATIC STUNTS are usually funny. They help people to limber up, use their hands and feet, or make noises that they might not ordinarily make. Dramatic stunts are fun to do and fun to watch.

THE OLD WITCH IS DEAD

Players sit in a circle. The first player says, "The Old Witch is dead." The player on his right says, "How did she die?"

The first player says, "Trying to fly." He waves his left arm up and down and keeps waving it as the second player turns to the player on his right and says, "The Old Witch is dead." The third player asks the question, and the second player answers, "Trying to fly," and makes the motion. This goes on until everyone in the circle is waving his left arm.

Then the first player says, "The Old Witch is dead."

"How did she die?" asks the second player.

"Patting her head," says the first player. He pats his head with his right hand and flies with his left. The questions and answers go on around the circle, and the motions are repeated. Soon everyone is patting his head with his right hand and waving with his left.

"The Old Witch is dead," says the first player again.

"How did she die?" asks the second player.

"Kicking up high," says the first player. He kicks one foot as high

as he can and keeps kicking while he continues to pat his head with his right hand and wave with his left. The questions and answers go around the circle. Soon everyone is patting, waving, and kicking.

No wonder the Old Witch died! Did she die laughing?

If a number of people are present, choose four or five to sit in front and do this stunt.

SMOKE GOES UP THE CHIMNEY

This is an action song. It can be sung on one note, or to a tune of your own. These are the words:

> Oh, you push the damper in,
> And you pull the damper out,
> And the smoke goes up the chimney
> Just the same. Just the same.
> And the smoke goes up the chimney just the same.

These are the motions. When you sing: *push the damper in,* push your right arm forward. *Pull the damper out,* pull your arm back. *Smoke goes up the chimney,* make spiral motion upward. First *just the same,* wave right arm to side. Second *just the same,* wave left arm to side.

Sing the song through with all the motions. Sing it again, but this time be quiet on *push the damper in.* Make motion in rhythm.

Repeat the song, being quiet on *push the damper in* and *pull the damper out.* Make motions.

Repeat the song, being quiet on *push the damper in, pull the damper out,* and the first *smoke goes up the chimney.* Make the motions.

Next time be quiet on the same phrases and also on the first *just the same.* Make motions. Then repeat, being quiet on all the phrases, including the second *just the same.* Make motions.

The last time you sing the song, the only words will be:

Oh, you (*motion*)

And you (*motion*)

And the (*motion*)

(*motion*) (*motion*)

And the (*motion*)

SANTA FORGETS

In this dramatic stunt, the audience makes every motion that SANTA *makes. A reader reads the story, pausing for the players' motions.*

Santa sat in his big armchair in front of the fire. He nodded his head. (*Droop head.*) He was half asleep. (*Breathe as if asleep.*) Faintly he heard Mrs. Santa say, "Why, you dear children, here are your treats. Good-by."

At these words, Santa sat up straight. (*Sit up straight.*) He yawned. (*Yawn.*) Then he looked at the clock. (*Look up.*)

"Great Scott!" he called. "Time to get going!" He jumped to his feet. (*Jump up.*) He reached up to the top shelf. (*Reach up.*) He got his hat and put it on his head. (*Put hat on head.*) He took one step to the right. (*Take one step to the right.*) He stood on his tiptoes. (*Stand on tiptoes.*)

"Where is my winter coat?" he called. He took one step to the left. (*Take step to left.*) He stood on his tiptoes. (*Stand on tiptoes.*)

40

"Mother," he called, "where is my winter coat?"

"Why do you want your winter coat?" Mrs. Santa asked.

"It's time to get started. I heard those poor children. They were here, asking for gifts! I should be at their homes, giving them gifts!"

"Now, Santa," his wife said. "Sit down. Please sit down."

Santa sat down. (*Sit down.*)

"Santa, you are all mixed up. This is Halloween. The children came here for 'tricks or treats.'"

"Oh!" said Santa, taking a deep breath. (*Take deep breath.*) "Oh, then happy Halloween! I guess I'd better pay attention. Then I'll know when it's Christmas." (*Sit up, wide awake.*)

I CAN'T PAY THE RENT

Before you do this melodrama, pinch a paper napkin in the center so that it looks like a bow. With the bow as your only property, you play all three characters in the melodrama, changing your voice each time you speak and changing the position of the bow.

VILLAIN *holds the bow like a mustache. Speaks in a low, sinister voice.*

GIRL *holds the bow on top of her head like a hair ribbon. Speaks in a high, timid voice.*

HERO *holds the bow like a necktie. Speaks slowly in a noble voice.*

VILLAIN. Knock. Knock.

GIRL. Who's there?

VILLAIN (*fiercely*). I have come for the rent.

GIRL (*desperately*). I can't pay the rent. I can't pay the rent. I can't pay the rent today.

VILLAIN (*determinedly*). You must pay the rent. You must pay the rent. You must pay the rent today.

GIRL (*more desperately*). I can't pay the rent. I can't pay the rent. I can't pay the rent today.

VILLAIN (*more fiercely*). You must pay the rent. You must pay the rent. You must pay the rent today.

(*Sound of hoofbeats off stage, made by beating hands on knees or table.*)

HERO (*nobly*). I'll pay the rent.

GIRL. My hero!

VILLAIN (*angrily*). Curses! Foiled again!

HALLOWEEN NIGHT

Before you read this story to your audience, explain to them that they are to make the sound effects. They are all Halloween sounds and should be as eerie as possible. Print the list of words which require sounds and put it where the audience can read it. Practice the words and sounds. Then read the story, pausing after the words on the list.

young girl—*eeeeek*

wind—*owwww*

owl—*whoooo*

rap—*knock, knock*

witch—*ha! ha!*

cat—*mew, mew*

young man—*ohooooooo*

Halloween ghost—*all the above noises at once, until the reader raises his hand for quiet.*

Alone in a cottage on a dark and stormy night sat a timid young girl (*eeeeek*). It was cold in the cottage, so she stirred up the fire on the hearth. But through the windows blew the wind (*owwww*). Outside was heard the long, low cry of the owl (*whoooo*).

She was not afraid, this timid young girl (*eeeeek*), until she heard a sound at the door — a rap (*knock, knock*).

"Who's there?" called the girl (*eeeeek*).

"It is I," croaked the old witch (*ha! ha!*). "Just I and my cat (*mew, mew*)."

"I don't like strangers on Halloween night," said the timid young girl (*eeeeek*).

"I don't like the wind (*owwww*) and the owl (*whoooo*)," said the old witch (*ha! ha!*). "Let me in and I'll tell your fortune."

"All right," said the young girl (*eeeeek*). "I need a fortune."

The young girl (*eeeeek*) opened the door, and in came the old witch (*ha! ha!*), the cat (*mew, mew*), the owl (*whoooo*), and the wind (*owwww*).

"Mmmmmmm," said the witch (*ha! ha!*), as she took the hand of the young girl (*eeeeek*). "Mmmmmmm, I see coming into your life a young man (*ohoooooo*)."

"Who?" asked the young girl (*eeeeek*).

"You'll see," answered the witch (*ha! ha!*).

Just then there was a rap (*knock, knock*).

"Come in!" cried the young girl (*eeeeek*).

There in the doorway stood a young man (*ohoooooo*). His face was covered by a wide-brimmed hat.

"I have come for you," said the young man (*ohoooooo*).

"Who are you, my prince?" sighed the timid young girl (*eeeeek*). He lifted his hat just a little.

"I knew it!" yelled the old witch (*ha! ha!*) and out of the window she flew with her cat (*mew, mew*) and the owl (*whoooo*) into the wind (*owwww*).

"Who are you?" again asked the timid young girl (*eeeeek*).

"I'm — " said the young man (*ohoooooo*), taking off his hat slowly, "I'm the Halloween ghost (*all noises*)."

ROUND AND ROUND AND ROUND

Characters

WITCH   PRINCE

PRINCESS   STORYTELLER

SCENE. *A castle tower. A chair represents the tower. In order to climb to the top of the tower, the actors go round and round many times. In order to come down from the tower, they go round the chair the other way. There is a stool nearby. The characters pantomime the action while the* STORYTELLER *reads the verses.*

Up to the tower the old Witch went,   (WITCH *climbs slowly*)
Round and round and round,
Round and round and round,
Round and round and round,
Round and round some more.
Over the ramparts the old Witch looked,   (*puts hand to eyes*)
Looked from mountains to the shore.   (*keeps looking*)
To the foot of the tower the Princess came,   (*comes to chair*)
Found herself a seat.   (*sits on stool*)
The young Prince saw her sitting there   (PRINCE *puts hands to
    eyes, sees* PRINCESS)
And knelt down at her feet.   (*kneels at her feet*)

The old Witch spied the pair,   (WITCH *looks horrified*)
Then gave a shriek   (*shriek*)
And started down.   (*starts down*)
Down the steps she came, down and down and down,
Down and down and down,
Down and down and down,
Down and down and down.

The Prince saw her sneaking up,   (WITCH *sneaks up behind
    pair;* PRINCE *jumps up*)
Saw her just in time.
He grabbed the Princess by the hand   (*grabs her hand*)
And started in to climb.   (PRINCE *and* PRINCESS *climb*)
Round and round and round they went,
Round and round and round,
Followed by the awful Witch,   (WITCH *follows, but can't quite
    catch them*)
Round and round and round,
Round and round and round.

When they reached the very top,   (*pant all out of breath*)
The old Witch slipped and fell.   (WITCH *starts to fall*)
Down and down and down she went,   (WITCH *goes down*)
Down and down and down,
Down and down and down,
Down and down pell-mell.
The young Prince sighed (*gives long sigh*), "Marry me, my dear."
     (PRINCE *and* PRINCESS *hold hands*)
"I'd like to, but I can't, up here."   (PRINCESS *holds out hands*)

So down from the tower the young pair came,
Down and down and down,
Down and down and down,
Down and down and down,
Down and down and down.
Their voices rang with joyous laughter.   (PRINCE *and* PRINCESS
     say, "Ha! Ha!")
They lived happily forever after.   (PRINCE *and* PRINCESS *say,*
     "Ha! Ha!")

THE SPLIT BALL

Characters

BUD UPSTREET, pitcher

BILL NELSON, reporter

SHORTY, catcher

GENTLEMAN FROM AUSTRALIA

OTHER VISITING GENTLEMEN

TWO FLASHLIGHT OPERATORS, who stand backstage

SCENE: *Practice field. The front stage is very dimly lighted. Across the back is a sheet or other lightweight curtain through which a light can shine. The success of the stunt depends upon the ability of the pitcher, catcher, and flashlight operators to coordinate their movements. The pitcher pantomimes a throw. When he says, "There," a flashlight operator turns on his light and makes it shine through the screen. The catcher pretends to catch the ball, and the light goes off. The movement of the ball may or may not resemble the flight of that kind of ball in a real game.*

(BUD *comes onto the stage, in front of the curtain.* BILL *steps up to him, followed by all the* VISITING GENTLEMEN.)

BILL. Hi, Bud.

BUD. Hi, Bill.

BILL (*turning to* VISITING GENTLEMEN). Gentlemen, I'd like you to meet Bud Upstreet, the greatest pitcher in America.

BUD. Oh, come on, Bill!

BILL. It's true. Bud, these gentlemen represent the World Wide Athletic Association. They wanted to see the greatest American pitcher, so I brought them right to you.

BUD. Well, I am flattered.

BILL. These are: Mr. Grossman of Australia, Mr. Blackwell of England, Mr. Lepere from France, Mr. Dimento from Italy. (*Add as many names and countries as you wish. Each shakes hands with* BUD *and then steps away.*)

GENTLEMAN FROM AUSTRALIA. Excuse me, sir. We have heard about

the many different ways that you pitch a ball. Would you mind demonstrating a few balls for us?

Bud. Glad to do what I can. Would you gentlemen like to be seated? (*Points to front row of seats.*)

Gentlemen. Thank you. Thank you. (*Seat themselves as* Bud *continues to talk.*)

Bud. Shorty.

Shorty (*appearing*). Yes, Bud.

Bud. These gentlemen want to see me throw a few balls. Mind catching?

Shorty. Glad to. (*Walks to opposite side of stage.*)

Bud. Gentlemen, this is Shorty McAdams.

Shorty and Gentlemen. How do you do?

Bud. Well, what shall I show them, Bill?

Bill (*standing behind* Shorty). Start with a fast ball.

Bud. O.K. A fast ball. There! (*Light darts across screen.* Gentlemen *cheer as* Shorty *catches it. They cheer after each catch.*)

Bill. A slow ball.

Bud. O.K. A slow ball. There! (*Light moves very slowly across screen.*)

Bill. A curve ball.

Bud. O.K. A curve ball. There! (*Light moves in fancy curve.*)

Bill. A knuckle ball. Gentlemen, that's a fooler.

Bud. O.K. A knuckle ball. There! (*Light goes in zigzag line.*)

BILL. A drop ball.

BUD. O.K. A drop ball. There! (*Light goes way up and then drops suddenly into* SHORTY'S *mits.*)

BILL. A sinker.

BUD. O.K. A sinker. There! (*Light glides along waist-high, then drops into* SHORTY'S *mits.*)

BILL. A floater.

BUD. O.K. A floater. There! (*Light goes up as if it's floating and comes into* SHORTY'S *hands gently.*)

BILL. How about a slider?

BUD. A slider. There! (*Light goes back and forth and slides into* SHORTY'S *mits.*)

GENTLEMAN FROM AUSTRALIA (*rising*). Pardon me, sir. I have heard about a split ball. Will you please show us a split ball?

BILL. Can you do a split ball, Bud?

BUD. Certainly. A split ball. There! (*The two flashlights start together. They seem to separate, one showing above the other on the screen. Then, just as they near* SHORTY, *they come together.*)

(GENTLEMEN *cheer.*)

Tableaux

A TABLEAU is a picture made by a group of persons who stand silent and motionless in appropriate positions.

For a program, there is usually a reader who explains a series of people pictures, or tableaux. The curtain is opened for each picture and closed after a minute or so. Often there is a chorus or other music while the scene is being changed.

A tableaux program may be given with one general rehearsal, or sometimes none. But every actor must know exactly where he stands for each scene. Actors must take positions quickly to avoid delay between scenes. Property men must know exactly where each piece of scenery should be placed.

Costuming for a tableau may be simple. However, if you have costumes, you can put on more elaborate programs. Some of these may represent "Christmas Around the World," "Great Moments in History," "Songs from Long Ago," "Copies of Famous Pictures," or "UNICEF (United Nations Children's Fund) Helps Around the World" (or the Red Cross, your church, or some other world-wide organization).

THE FAMILY TREE

As curtain opens on each tableau, the reader describes the characters.

Our family were all pioneers.
That's why they lived for years and years.
A jolly lass was Aunt McGuffy;
Very sweet, but slightly stuffy.
(Tableau shows naturally thin girl, wearing a large dress stuffed with pillows.)

Uncle Lank was full of vim.
Aunt Flora helped him keep in trim.
(Tableau shows UNCLE LANK *with bowl on his head.* AUNT FLORA *is trimming his hair at edge of bowl.)*

Aunt Eliz counted every penny.
It was easy. She hadn't any.
(Tableau shows AUNT ELIZ *with empty purse upside down.)*

Uncle Nat was strong and bold.
He never seemed to fear the cold.
(Tableau shows UNCLE NAT, *bundled in coat and blankets. Around his head is wrapped a scarf so that only his nose shows.)*

And now I'm sure it's plain to see.
There were many nuts on our family tree.
(Tableau shows all relatives. They may be grouped three in front row, two in second row. Each holds a nut, dangling from a ribbon.)

Write descriptive verses about other relatives. Add these new verses and new tableaux to the program.

Build a large frame to represent the margins of a page of a book, or let partially drawn curtains frame your pictures. Use a curtain backdrop.

Tell something about each story. Show the tableau. Ask the audience to guess the names of the characters and tell in what book they appear.

You can use the book descriptions given here; or you can choose other books, design appropriate tableaux, and write your own descriptions.

This friend was a young man when I first met him. He hated work and he hated to have his wife scold him because he did not work.

He liked to hunt. One day he took his gun upon his shoulder and went to the Catskill Mountains. Strange things happened, after which he fell asleep for twenty years. When he woke up and returned to his home, he found things had changed considerably.

(*Tableau of* RIP VAN WINKLE. *From* Rip Van Winkle, *by Washington Irving.*)

This friend is a little girl. She lived with her grandfather on a mountain in Switzerland. She loved to pick gay flowers while she spent long hours watching the goats with her friend Peter.

(*Tableau of* HEIDI *and* PETER. *From* Heidi, *by Johanna Spyri.*)

This friend is a mischievous puppet with a long nose. He little appreciated the kindness of his good father, who had carved him out of wood. A good friend at last taught him that he must think of others before he could become a real boy.

(*Tableau of* Pinocchio *and the* Blue Fairy. *From* Adventures of Pinocchio, *by Carlo Lorenzini.*)

This friend was sitting on the grass, wondering if she should get up and pick daisies, when she saw a White Rabbit wearing a waistcoat and holding a large gold watch. She heard him say, "Dear, dear! I'm late again!" and then she saw him pop right down a rabbit hole. She was so surprised that she popped right in after him.

(*Tableau of* Alice *sitting on grass with* White Rabbit *standing near her looking at his gold watch. From* Alice's Adventures in Wonderland, *by Lewis Carroll.*)

These friends lived in a pleasant little town on the banks of the Mississippi. As a rule, they enjoyed life in spite of school and lickings. But once they decided that they were not appreciated at home and stole away to Jackson's Island to become pirates. However, homesickness soon got the better of them.

(*Tableau of* Tom Sawyer, Huck Finn, *and* Joe Harper *around campfire. From* Adventures of Tom Sawyer, *by Mark Twain.*)

53

THE PILGRIM STORY

After READER *describes a tableau, curtain opens showing scene.*

On December 21, 1620, a group of one hundred and two English men, women, and children landed on the Massachusetts shore. Some of them were merchants, some were farmers and tradespeople, a few were servants. All were Pilgrims, searching for a land where they could worship as they pleased, rear their children in their own traditions, and make an honest living. Their first act upon landing was to thank God, who had guided them on their perilous journey.

(*Tableau of* PILGRIMS, *some kneeling, some standing. Men have hats off. Heads are bowed. Plymouth Rock in background.*)

The first winter in the new land was a hard one for the Pilgrims. Nearly everyone was sick. At one time, only six people were strong enough to walk. These six people had to care for the sick, hunt for food, cut wood, and be on the lookout for savages, men or beasts.

The Pilgrims knew that they were in Indian country, because upon their arrival they had found Indian baskets, filled with corn. But December changed into January, and no Indians had been seen.

Then one day a tall and powerful Indian warrior, well armed with bow and arrows, suddenly appeared. Fearlessly he walked down the street of the village and into the common house where the Pilgrim fathers were meeting. He extended his arm, and then to the surprise of everyone, uttered one word in English: "Welcome."

(*Tableau of* PILGRIM FATHERS *at table, some seated, some standing.* INDIAN *stands with backstage arm outstretched.*)

The Indian was Samoset. He told the Pilgrims that the abandoned cornfields had belonged to a tribe of Indians, all of whom had died of a sickness. He promised to come again and to bring with him Squanto, an Indian who had traveled across the sea.

Samoset did return and bring Squanto. From them the Pilgrims learned many things, especially how to plant the new food — corn — by putting fish in the bottom of the hole.

(*Tableau of* INDIAN *showing* PILGRIMS *how to plant corn.*)

When spring came, only fifty of the one hundred and two Pilgrims remained alive. These fifty grew strong. They were able to kill game, catch sea food, and plant crops. Every man, woman, and child worked in the fields. They planted six acres with seeds brought from England — wheat, barley, and peas — and twenty acres of corn.

They built houses much like those they had had in England — houses made of hewn board with thatched roofs. By fall there were eleven houses — seven private homes and four public houses.

Harvest time came. The English crops amounted to almost nothing. But the corn crop was good. Besides corn, the Pilgrims had sea food, wild game, berries, and fruit.

(*Tableau of* PILGRIMS *with harvest and game.*)

The Pilgrims were thankful for more than food. They had made peace with the Indians. They had beaver skins for trade. There had

been no sickness for months. It was time, the Pilgrims said, to have
a holiday for thanksgiving. They invited the Indians as guests.

As the day of the holiday grew near, men went into the woods for
game. Women cooked and cooked. At last the dinner was ready. There
were venison, roast duck, roast goose, clams and other shellfish, eels,
and wild plums, and berries for dessert.

No mention is made in the early records of turkey, cranberries, or
pumpkin pie. But the Pilgrims had plenty to eat without them.

Indians and Pilgrims gathered around the ladened table. Then they
paused to thank God for all his gifts.

(*Tableau of* Pilgrims *standing with bowed heads around a ladened
table.* Indians *stand nearby. All remain in position as* Chorus *sings
"Faith of Our Fathers."*)

Skits

A SKIT is a dramatized joke or funny situation with a snapper line at the end. You don't need to memorize all the lines in a skit, but you must get the snapper line across to the audience. Speak loudly. Make plenty of motions. Have fun with a skit.

IT'S A GIFT

Characters

JANE	SUE
PHYLLIS	IRENE
BARBARA	PROPERTY MAN

SCENE: *Girl's room. Near center stage is a small table on which there is a mirror, a card, and a box containing a wild-colored scarf.*

JANE (*enters, picks up card on box, and reads*). "Merry Christmas to Jane from Irene." (*Opens box.*) What do you know? A Christmas gift from Irene. Well, this is a surprise! (*Holds up scarf.*) Mmmm — Wonder how I can use it. (*She holds it to her neckline, ties it around her hair, holds it at her waistline. As she goes through the poses, she looks in the mirror and shows disgust.*) Really, I don't think these colors do much for me. But it might look all right on Phyllis. I know! I'll surprise her with a valentine gift. (*Puts scarf back into box. Exits.*)

(PROPERTY MAN *walks across stage with sign: Valentine Day.*)

PHYLLIS (*enters, picks up valentine, and reads*). "To Phyllis from Jane." Well, what a surprise! A valentine gift from Jane. (*Opens package.*) A scarf! (*She goes through the same motions Jane did.*) I don't think these colors do much for me. It might look all right on Barbara. I know! I'll give it to her for a graduation gift. (*She puts scarf back into box. Exits.*)

(PROPERTY MAN *crosses stage with sign: Graduation Day.*)

BARBARA (*enters and reads card*). "Happy graduation to Barbara from Phyllis." Well, what a surprise! I never expected to receive a gift from Phyllis. (*Opens gift.*) A scarf! (*She tries it in various ways, making remarks.*) I'm afraid it doesn't do much for me. But it might look all right on Sue. I know! I'll give it to Sue for her birthday. (*Puts scarf into box. Exits.*)

(PROPERTY MAN *crosses stage with sign: Sue's Birthday.*)

SUE (*enters and reads card*). "Happy birthday from Barbara." Well, what a surprise! (*Opens box.*) A scarf. *Mmmm* — Not quite my type. (*Tries to wear it different ways.*) You know, I think Irene might like this. I'il give it to her for Christmas. (*Puts scarf into box. Exits.*)

(PROPERTY MAN *crosses stage with sign: Christmas.*)

IRENE (*enters and reads card*). "To Irene from Sue." How sweet of Sue to remember me. (*Opens box.*) A scarf! Just the kind I've always wanted! (*Puts it on. Looks in mirror.*) I love it! Funny, though, it's a lot like the one I gave Jane last Christmas. But who cares? I love it. And it's a gift!

(BOYS *putting on the skit can use a hideous tie for a gift, or they can mimic girls. The skit can start with any holiday.*)

58

A SPOT OF ONION TEA
Characters

Mrs. Knight   Darry Knight, a son
Clara Knight, a daughter   Mrs. Leary, a neighbor

Scene. *The kitchen. On the table are trays covered with napkins, empty creamer and sugar, empty coffee pot. On a small table is a telephone. Off stage women are singing. A record may be used.*

Mrs. Knight. Oh, I do hope Darry comes soon with those groceries.

Clara. No rush. The women are still singing.

Mrs. Knight. But it's time to serve refreshments. And Darry isn't here with the cream, sugar, and instant coffee.

Clara. Everything else is ready.

Mrs. Knight. I know. I know. But Darry said he would stop at Hansen's right after school and bring home the groceries. He should be here by now.

Mrs. Leary (*entering*). Mrs. Knight, we are ready for refreshments.

Mrs. Knight. Oh, Mrs. Leary, will you ask the ladies to sing one more song? We aren't quite ready.

Mrs. Leary. Certainly. (*Exits. Singing continues.*)

Clara. Why don't you call Mr. Hansen? If Darry forgot to go, I'll rush down and get the groceries.

Mother. Good idea. (*Goes to phone. Dials.*) Hello, Mr. Hansen. This is Mrs. Knight. Has Darry been in your store this afternoon? He just left with Tom Watkins? They both had to stay after school? Oh, he did seem in a rush? Good! Thank you. Good-by. (*Hangs up.*) He's on his way — with the groceries!

Mrs. Leary (*entering*). Are you ready now, Mrs. Knight?

Mrs. Knight. Almost. Could you sing one more song?

Mrs. Leary. Certainly. (*Exits. Singing continues.*)

Mrs. Knight. Oh, dear! Oh, dear! I've never been so embarrassed in my life!

CLARA. Buck up, Mother. It could be worse.

MRS. KNIGHT. How? Just tell me how it could be worse.

DARRY (*running in*). Here they are, Mom! (*Hands her package.*) Did I make it in time?

MRS. KNIGHT. Not quite. Almost. (*Reaches in bag. Takes out articles without looking at them.*) Here, Clara, make some coffee. (*Hands her jar of mustard.*) Darry, fill the cream pitcher. (*Hands him catsup.*) I'll fill the sugar bowl. (*Opens bag.*) Onions! (*Looks around.*) Catsup! Mustard! Darry!

DARRY. I must have got Tom's bag. He's going on a picnic. (*They stand bewildered, holding catsup, mustard, onions.*)

MRS. LEARY (*entering*). Shall we sing one more song?

MRS. KNIGHT. Please do. Then ask the ladies if they'd like some catsup or some mustard in their spot of onion tea.

JUNK, VALUABLE JUNK!

Characters

AUNT FLORA   MOM
SPUD

SCENE: *Spud's room with desk, dresser, and two chairs.* AUNT FLORA *is busy taking things from Spud's desk and putting them into a carton.*

SPUD (*entering*). Hi, Aunt Flora! What are you doing?

AUNT FLORA. I'm cleaning your room.

SPUD. That's nice. (*Looks at desk.*) Say, what happened? Where's my doorknob? Where's my junk?

AUNT FLORA (*indicating carton*). Your junk's right here. Now, take this out to the curb.

SPUD. Out to the curb? Aunt Flora, what do you mean?

AUNT FLORA. Exactly what I said. I want these things out in the trash can before your mother gets home. (*She starts to wind string which extends from desk drawer. She keeps winding and winding.*)

SPUD. Ah, Aunt Flora, Mom doesn't mind these things. Just look. (*Picks up articles from carton.*) Here's a fish hook. (AUNT FLORA *nods, unimpressed.*) And copper wire. (*She nods again.*) And a doorknob.

AUNT FLORA. Yes, I recognize a doorknob.

SPUD. Aunt Flora, a doorknob is valuable!

AUNT FLORA (*still winding string into ball*). Ummmmm—

SPUD. Did you ever live in a house without a doorknob?

AUNT FLORA. Well, no.

SPUD. You don't want to throw away a doorknob. You might need one some day — say ten years from now.

AUNT FLORA. I know that I don't need a doorknob. Now throw this junk away. (SPUD *reluctantly picks up carton.*) And here, take this too. (*Tosses string into box.*)

SPUD. Aunt Flora, that's string! (*She nods.*) Mom never throws away string. (*She motions him out. He exits.*)

AUNT FLORA (*dusting*). Junk, junk, junk. (*Opens box on desk.*) Stones. No!

SPUD (*re-entering*). Aunt Flora, please don't touch my rocks! Say, I know what we could throw away. (*Opens dresser drawer.*)

AUNT FLORA. Spud, don't touch that drawer! I just put your things in order.

SPUD. But it's full of junk — stuff I never use. Here's a tie clip.

AUNT FLORA. A tie clip's valuable — if you ever wear a tie. And it doesn't take up much room.

SPUD. As much room as a fish hook. And this corduroy shirt. I never wear that. And— (*He continues to pull out shorts, pajamas, etc., as* AUNT FLORA *protests.*)

MOM (*entering*). Spud! Flora!

SPUD. Mom!

AUNT FLORA. Sister!

MOM. Oh, it's good to be home! Flora, I brought you a little gift. (*Hands* AUNT FLORA *an elaborately wrapped box.*)

AUNT FLORA. Oh, thank you! (*She sits down and starts to undo the ribbon very carefully.* SPUD *smiles, knowing she is going to save it.*)

MOM (*sitting down and opening her shopping bag*). And Spud, I found a pretty rock, just outside the fort. (*Hands him rock.*)

SPUD. Thanks, Mom. It's sure a conglomerate!

MOM. And guess what else I found, just outside the house, a doorknob! You never know when you'll need a doorknob—maybe ten years from now. (AUNT FLORA *looks up startled. Sighs. Continues to open gift.*)

SPUD. Thanks, Mom. Look what I've got for you. (*Pulls from pocket ball of string which* AUNT FLORA *had carefully wound and thrown away.*)

MOM. String, all wound up! How nice! Flora, isn't he the most understanding boy? (AUNT FLORA *starts to speak, chokes, and just nods.*)

RULER OF ALL — BUT ONE

Characters

GLOOSKAP, god of Algonquin
  Indians

CHIEF EAGLE EYE

CHIEF DEER FOOT

CHIEF BEAR CLAW

CHIEF SWIFT ARROW

CHIEF RED FEATHER

WASIS, a baby

OTHER INDIANS

MEDICINE MEN

SCENE: *A council fire.* GLOOSKAP *stands right stage.* INDIAN CHIEFS *stand left stage. Between them are seated other* INDIANS, MEDICINE MEN, *and* WASIS. WASIS *is in the center.*

GLOOSKAP (*extending backstage hand*). I am Glooskap, god of the Algonquin Indians.

CHIEF EAGLE EYE (*advancing and extending backstage hand*). Welcome, Glooskap, god of the Algonquin Indians. (*He stands back of seated* INDIANS *as* CHIEF DEER FOOT *advances.*)

CHIEF DEER FOOT (*extending backstage hand*). Welcome, Glooskap. It was you who overcame winter.

GLOOSKAP. Yes, it was I, Glooskap, who overcame winter.

63

(CHIEF DEER FOOT *stands near* CHIEF EAGLE EYE *as* CHIEF BEAR CLAW *advances.*)

CHIEF BEAR CLAW. Welcome, Glooskap! It was you who made the barren land fertile.

GLOOSKAP. Yes, it was I, Glooskap, who made the barren land fertile.

(CHIEF BEAR CLAW *stands near* CHIEF DEER FOOT *as* CHIEF SWIFT ARROW *advances.*)

CHIEF SWIFT ARROW (*raising backstage hand*). Welcome, Glooskap. It was you who overcame the witches, ghosts, and evil spirits which lived on earth before man came.

GLOOSKAP. Yes, I, Glooskap, control everything. I control the spirits of this world and of the worlds to come. I control the fish of the seas and the rivers, the birds of the air, the beasts of the fields and forests. I control every man, woman, and child. Everyone and everything must do as I command. (CHIEF SWIFT ARROW *stands near* CHIEF BEAR CLAW.)

CHIEF RED FEATHER (*advances, falls on knees, and bows*). Worthy Master, may I speak?

GLOOSKAP. Rise and speak.

CHIEF RED FEATHER. Worthy Master, I know one creature who will not come when you call.

GLOOSKAP. Impossible! I am Glooskap! Who can withstand my power?

CHIEF RED FEATHER. I have a baby. Wasis is twelve moons old. He can walk, but he will not come when he is called.

GLOOSKAP. A baby? Nothing could be easier than to make a baby mind the great Glooskap.

CHIEF RED FEATHER. But, Master, you do not have a child. You do not know my baby Wasis. There is one creature who will not come when you call.

GLOOSKAP. Nonsense! (CHIEF RED FEATHER *joins other chiefs.* GLOOS-KAP *claps hands. Commands.*) Wasis, come to me! (*Folds arms and*

64

waits. WASIS, *who is eating maple sugar, looks at* GLOOSKAP. *Smiles.*)
Ah, Wasis, you are a child of the forest. I shall whistle for you.
(*Whistles like bird.* WASIS *looks at him.*) Wasis, you will come to me
when you hear the music of your fathers. (*Sings short song.* WASIS *eats
candy. Smiles.*) Wasis! I command you to come to me!

WASIS (*frightened*). *Waaaaa!* (*Continues to cry.*)

GLOOSKAP. Wasis, you have an evil spirit in you. The medicine men
must rid you of it. Beat the drums!

(INDIANS *beat drums.* GLOOSKAP *and* MEDICINE MEN *run around
stage, swaying up and down and yelling.*)

WASIS (*crying louder than ever*). *Waaaaa!*

GLOOSKAP. Stop! (*Drums and* MEDICINE MEN *are quiet.* WASIS *cries
louder than ever.*) Wasis, stop crying! (WASIS *continues to yell.*) I give
up. I am ruler of all but one. (*Points to* WASIS.) You, Wasis! (*Exits in
anger.*)

WASIS (*watches* GLOOSKAP *until he disappears, then smiles*). *Goooo!*

Plays

THERE ARE many kinds of plays. A play may be funny or sad, fantastic or realistic, short or long, zany or beautiful, simple or complicated. Choose a play you like; then act it out. You can put on a play on the spur of the moment. Or you can produce a more formal play which requires careful planning and rehearsals.

To enact a spur-of-the-moment play, reread a story that you like. Then act it out. You don't need to memorize lines. Make them up as you go along. Use anything you happen to have for costumes, properties, or scenery. Or do without any of them.

You can use a story you know well. You can add lines to the pantomime plays in this book (pages 26-32). You can use some of the puppet plays (pages 100-154). Or you can imagine a situation and make up a play of your own.

If, after you have gone through your impromptu play, you think it is interesting enough, ask members of your family or neighbors to be your audience while you repeat the performance.

In putting on a formal play, the first thing to do after selecting it is to plan the action. Aim for balance on the stage, avoiding any grouping that crowds one side leaving the opposite side empty. Bring action to the front — downstage. Try not to turn your back to the audience.

Study your character, deciding how he would talk, walk, sit, and stand. Then learn your lines.

When doing any kind of acting, remember that you are playing the part of a character all the time — when you are listening as well as when you are talking. Never drop out of character.

Speak your lines clearly and more slowly than ordinarily. Speak loud enough to be heard in every corner of the room.

Put all of yourself into your acting. Soon you will forget that you are you and will have fun being someone else for a short time.

66

TIT FOR TAT

Characters

FRED   CHUCK

ECHO

SCENE: *A glen.* FRED *is on stage.* ECHO *is hidden.*

FRED (*yells*). Stop it!

ECHO. Stop it.

FRED. I hate you!

ECHO. Hate you.

FRED. Leave me alone!

ECHO. Me alone.

CHUCK (*entering*). What are you doing, Fred?

FRED. That echo makes me sick. Always hollering at me. (*Yells.*) Always picking on me.

ECHO. On me.

CHUCK. I like the echo. Listen. (*Calls.*) Hello.

ECHO. Hello.

CHUCK. How are you?

ECHO. Are you?

CHUCK. Come over.

ECHO. Over.

FRED. Yeah, he's nice to you. (*Yells.*) Why does he pick on me?

ECHO. On me.

CHUCK. You yell at him, so he yells at you. I like him, so he's nice to me. When you get mad, you always start something.

FRED. I start something. How do you like that? Want to make something of it? (*Rolls up sleeves. Starts toward* CHUCK.)

ECHO. Of it.

CHUCK. No, thanks! (*Exits.*)

FRED (*thoughtfully*). What does he mean? When I get mad, I start something. I yell at him, so he yells at me. (*Pauses.*) If I'm nice to him — (*Smiles, catching on.*) He means it's tit for tat. (*Louder.*) Ohhhh —

ECHO. Ohhhh —

(FRED *smiles. Makes a "Hi, Pal!" gesture toward* ECHO. *Exits.*)

THE OLD WOMAN AND THE TRAMP
Characters

OLD WOMAN   TRAMP

SCENE: *The kitchen of* OLD WOMAN. *A fireplace is seen right front. A table, with a chair drawn up at either side, stands center stage. At back of stage is a cupboard containing tablecloth, silverware, candlesticks with candles in them, napkins, a bowl for barley, dish for meat, bread, pitcher for milk, plates, and glasses. A kettle with a big spoon in it and a jar of water stand near the fireplace, where logs are laid over an electric light which can be turned on to resemble a glowing fire.* OLD WOMAN *is standing behind the table slicing vegetables.*

(*Loud knocking is heard at door.*)

OLD WOMAN. My goodness! Who is that? (*Starts to look out of window, then returns to table.*) Well, whoever it is, I'd better put this food away. (*Puts vegetables into dish and puts dish into cupboard. Returns to table.*) No use looking too well off. Better let people think I have too little rather than too much.

(*Knocking comes again.*)

68

OLD WOMAN. Goodness! How could anyone tell that I was home? I'll be as quiet as a mouse. (*Sits down, folds hands.*)

TRAMP (*outside*). Old Woman, please let me come in! (OLD WOMAN *sits still.*) Please, Old Woman! It's going to rain. (OLD WOMAN *sits still.*) Please, please, Old Woman! Please let me just step in. It's cold, and the rain is coming.

OLD WOMAN. Now how did he know I was here? (*Goes to door.*)

TRAMP (*entering*). Good afternoon, madam. What a cheery home you have!

(OLD WOMAN *looks around the room, surprised to hear it called cheery. While she is looking the other way,* TRAMP *comes downstage and stands near fire.*)

TRAMP. May I come in?

OLD WOMAN. I guess you are in! Where did you come from, may I ask? (*She comes downstage, too.*)

TRAMP. I came from east of the sun and west of the moon. I've seen all the world except this little forest. Soon I shall return home.

OLD WOMAN. What do you want here?

TRAMP. Food and shelter for one night.

OLD WOMAN. Food? What makes you think I have food? And why should I give you shelter?

TRAMP. I'll answer the second question first. You should give me shelter because human beings should help one another.

OLD WOMAN. Help one another, indeed! I can give you shelter. But how can you help me?

TRAMP. How can I help you? That's related to your first question. You asked about food. Remember?

OLD WOMAN. I remember.

TRAMP. I see you have a fireplace.

OLD WOMAN. Yes, I have a fireplace.

TRAMP. I see you have wood. (*Goes to fireplace.*) See? In a minute we'll have a jolly fire. (*Blows on fire. Electric light is turned on. Fire glows.*) See?

OLD WOMAN. What good is a jolly fire, burning up my wood?

TRAMP. You have no food, or none to share. But I have a nail. I'll gladly share that.

OLD WOMAN. A nail to share? For what?

TRAMP. For nail soup.

OLD WOMAN. Nail soup! I never heard of such a thing!

TRAMP. Just the same, it could be true.

      Even if it's new to you.

Get me the kettle, Old Woman.

(OLD WOMAN *hands* TRAMP *a kettle with big spoon in it.* TRAMP *pours water into it from jar.*)

TRAMP. Today you heard about nail soup.

OLD WOMAN. For the first time in my life.

TRAMP. Today you shall see nail soup. (*He drops nail into soup and puts kettle on fire. He stirs soup.*)

OLD WOMAN. Nail soup! Certainly every poor person should know how to make nail soup. I'd like to learn to make it, too. (*She watches him intently.*)

TRAMP (*turning*). This usually makes very good soup. But this soup may be a little thin. I've been using the same nail all week. A little barley would improve the soup. But —

I'm thankful for the things I get.

For what I lack, I never fret.

OLD WOMAN. A little barley? Come to think of it, I do have a little barley. (*She goes to cupboard.* TRAMP *smiles knowingly while her back is turned.* OLD WOMAN *returns to fireplace and hands barley to* TRAMP.) There!

TRAMP (*pouring barley into soup and returning dish to* OLD WO-MAN). Now that does make elegant nail soup. (*Stirs.*) This nail soup is almost like the nail soup that I had at the squire's house. Only the squire had some vegetables in his nail soup. But —

I'm thankful for the things I get.

For what I lack, I never fret.

OLD WOMAN (*getting excited*). Nail soup like the squire had? Well, we, too, can have soup like the squire's. (*Goes to cupboard and fetches bowl containing vegetables. Hands bowl to* TRAMP.) There! If the squire has vegetables in his nail soup, so shall we!

TRAMP (*taking vegetables and putting them into kettle*). Elegant! Elegant! (*Returns bowl to* OLD WOMAN.) Only one person has better nail soup — the king. The king has meat in his soup. But a poor man can't expect to eat like a king.

(Old Woman *turns as he continues to talk, goes to cupboard, returns empty vegetable bowl to shelf, and brings back dish with meat.*)

Tramp. So —

I'm thankful for the things I get.

For what I lack, I never fret.

Old Woman. Today we shall eat like kings. See, I, too, have meat for our nail soup.

Tramp (*taking dish with meat*). Nail soup with meat! Truly a royal dish. (*Puts meat into kettle. Returns bowl to* Old Woman.) In fact, today we might dine like a king and queen — if we had a tablecloth, silverware, milk, and bread. But a royal dish we have, if not a royal setting.

(Tramp *stirs soup.* Old Woman *goes to cupboard for tablecloth. Comes to table as* Tramp *is talking.*)

Tramp. But —

I'm thankful for the things I get.

For what I lack, I never fret.

Old Woman. See! See! I, too, have a cloth. Come help me. (Tramp *helps her spread cloth.* Old Woman *runs back and forth to cupboard.*) And silverware, candlesticks, bread, and butter! (*Excitedly and quickly she sets table. Then pauses to look at it.*) And nail soup!

Tramp. Nail soup fit for a king!

Old Woman. My good fellow, how can I thank you? I am so glad that you came this way! (Tramp *smiles. Goes to fireplace while she is talking. Scoops nail out of soup. Returns to table.*) You taught me how to make nail soup — such an economical dish! Nail soup fit for a king!

Tramp. I'll put this little nail away

To make more soup another day. (*Puts nail in pocket.*)

Now, my good woman, if you'll be seated, I shall serve you. (*Goes behind her chair.*) Your Majesty, shall we dine?

(Old Woman *is seated, feeling every inch a queen.*)

DOG GONE
Characters

Mrs. Jenks	Ben, Joe's friend
Joe Jenks, her son	Mrs. Lloyd, a neighbor
Ruth Jenks, her daughter	Laundryman
Mr. O'Brien, a policeman	Mack, a small dog

Scene: *The Jenks' home. Outside door is center back; kitchen door, right; den door, left. Mrs. Jenks is phoning, right center.*

Mrs. Jenks. No, honestly, you don't bake it at all. Just put it into the refrigerator. It looks like fruit cake. In a way it is fruit —

Joe (*entering excitedly*). Mom! Mom! Mack's gone. (*Sees she is phoning.*) I'm sorry, Mom. Excuse me, Mom. I have to talk to you. Mack's gone. (*Rushes around room whistling, looking under table, chairs, etc.*)

Mrs. Jenks. Excuse me, Ann. Joe seems upset. No, it's not his stomach.

Joe. Mom, it's important!

Mrs. Jenks (*into phone*). Don't worry. He'll be all right. I'll call back. (*Hangs up. Turns to Joe.*) What's the matter, Joe? You know I don't like to be interrupted when I'm phoning. Sit down, or at least stand still. Tell me what's wrong.

RUTH (*entering*). Hi! What's new? I'm going to phone Sally.

JOE. No, no. Just wait a minute, Sis. I've got to phone.

RUTH. Well, so do I. You weren't using the phone when I came in. (*Takes up phone and dials.*)

MRS. JENKS. Please, Joe, tell me what's the matter.

JOE. I told you. Mack is gone. I put him in the yard this morning. I locked the gate. The gate is still locked, but Mack is gone.

RUTH (*on phone while others are talking*). Oh, no! Who says? (*And so on.*)

MRS. JENKS. Are you sure? Now let's see. He was in the yard this morning when I was talking to Mrs. Lloyd.

JOE. Mrs. Lloyd?

MRS. JENKS. Why, yes. The phone rang. I came in. I counted the laundry. The phone rang. (JOE *nods. He is polite but very impatient as she rambles on.*) Then the laundryman came. I tied up the laundry. He said, "Lots of wash this week." I said —

JOE. Excuse me, Mom. I've got to use the phone.

MRS. JENKS. But why, Joe? Why the phone? Mack'll come home. All dogs come home. (RUTH *is still jabbering, "She's nuts," etc.*)

JOE. Oh, Mom, she doesn't need the phone. I do!

MRS. JENKS. Why, Joe?

JOE. Why? You know why! The Lloyds! The Lloyds said they'd call the pound the next time Mack got out. I have to call the dog pound!

RUTH (*to* JOE). What did you say? Mack's at the dog pound? (*Into phone.*) Hold it.

JOE. Mack's lost. He might be at the dog pound. (MRS. JENKS *sits down. Starts to mend.*)

RUTH (*into phone*). O.K., Sally. 'By. (*To* JOE.) Here's the phone. (*He starts to dial.* RUTH *crosses to chair. Plumps down.*) Wonder where Mack is. The dog pound? Say! Remember? The Lloyds said —(*Doorbell rings.*) There's the doorbell. Maybe someone has found Mack.

JOE (*phoning*). Hello. Hello. The dog pound? I dialed wrong? Oh, no! (*Hangs up.*)

RUTH (*at door*). Hello, Ben. Joe, Ben's here. I'll try to get the pound for you. (*Goes to phone.*)

BEN (*coming downstage where* JOE *joins him*). What's the matter with you, Joe? Someone make you go to school on Saturday?

JOE. Mack's gone.

BEN. That's too bad. Think someone took him?

JOE. No, I'm afraid he got out and the Lloyds turned him in to the pound. Can't get the pound.

RUTH. Line's busy.

BEN. I know! I'll go down to the *News*. Maybe someone saw Mack in a strange place and called the *News*.

JOE. Thanks, Ben. (*Doorbell rings.*) Oh, someone's at the door. (*Goes to door with* BEN.)

MR. O'BRIEN. Hello, Joe. Hello, Ben. Are you leaving?

BEN. Yes, sir. (*Exits.*)

JOE. Come in, Mr. O'Brien.

MR. O'BRIEN. Thank you, Joe. (*Comes downstage.*) Hello, Ruth. Good afternoon, Mrs. Jenks. (JOE *starts to phone.*) I've had a complaint.

JOE (*rushing up and interrupting*). Please, sir, let me explain. I locked the gate this morning. Honest I did. I don't know how he got

out. I'll pay for any damage he did. Just give me time, officer. Just give him another chance.

Mr. O'Brien. I'm sorry, Joe. I don't know what you are talking about.

Joe. You don't? Really? Swell! If I can just get the phone!

Mrs. Jenks. Officer, Mack is missing.

Mr. O'Brien. Too bad. Nice dog, Mack! I'll look for him. About my other business — (Joe *starts to dial.*) I've had a complaint about an odor from the sewer. Have you noticed it?

Mrs. Jenks. Oh, no, officer.

Mr. O'Brien. Thank you, Mrs. Jenks. Good-by, Ruth. Good-by Joe. I'll look for Mack. (*Goes to door.* Ruth *rises to open it for him.*)

Ruth, Joe, Mrs. Jenks. Thank you, sir. Good-by.

Ruth (*looking out door*). Joe, here comes Mrs. Lloyd!

Joe. Mrs. Lloyd! Oh, no! I'd better not call the pound now. I'm vanishing, disappearing, vamoosing. Call the pound if you can. (*Exits through den door.*)

Ruth (*opening door for* Mrs. Lloyd). Good afternoon, Mrs. Lloyd.

Mrs. Jenks (*rising as* Mrs. Lloyd *comes downstage*). Good afternoon, Mrs. Lloyd. So nice of you to come over.

Mrs. Lloyd. I just had to come.

Ruth (*choking*). Yes, we thought you had to come.

Mrs. Lloyd. You did? Why did you think I had to come?

Mrs. Jenks (*interrupting*). We thought you'd like to taste my new fruit cake. It isn't baked. You put it into the refrigerator. Come into the kitchen. I'll show you. (*They exit.* Ruth *goes to den door.*)

Ruth. All clear, Joe.

Joe (*entering*). She gone?

Ruth. Not far. (*Crosses to window.*)

Joe. Then I'll phone. (*Picks up phone.*)

Ruth. Say, a truck's stopping.

Joe. Dog-catcher's truck?

Ruth. No, laundry truck. (*Bell rings.* Ruth *goes to door.*)

JOE. Mom sent the laundry.

RUTH (*opening door*). Hello. Mom sent the laundry.

LAUNDRYMAN (*entering, carrying something wrapped in sheet*). I'll say she sent the laundry. (*Comes downstage.*) Including this! (*He lets* MACK *jump out of sheet.*)

RUTH and JOE. Mack! (*They fall on his neck.*)

WILDERNESS BIRTHDAY
Characters

ADA BARTLETT	MRS. BARTLETT
JOHNNIE APPLESEED	NED BARTLETT
MUTT, Johnnie's dog	

SCENE: *Near a brook in the Midwest, one hundred years ago.* ADA *is sitting, half dreaming.* JOHNNIE *and* MUTT *enter.* JOHNNIE *wears a burlap coffee-sack shirt, short, faded overalls, and a wide-brimmed cardboard hat. His legs are bare.*

JOHNNIE. Mind if we rest a bit?

ADA (*waking*). Oh, no. Is that your dog?

JOHNNIE. Mine? No, he's his own, I guess. He was kicked most to death by a good-for-nothing master. So I paid a few pennies to save his

life, and we've been traveling together ever since. But he's still afeared of most everybody.

ADA. Not of you.

JOHNNIE. No, I've taken care of him. Besides, I'm always friends with everyone. That's the way I feel, and of course all creatures, dumb animals, Indians, children, and sometimes even grownups understand if you feel that way. (*Looks up.*) You have fine company here. That redbird is my favorite. Birds don't come with a prettier song. Still, it's nice to meet a little girl. You and your folks must be new in these parts.

ADA. We've been here more than a year. We came all the way from Boston. It seems like a thousand years ago.

JOHNNIE. I'm from Boston, too. But by your count I left there a million years ago. Well, how are you making out on the frontier? *Hmm,* I reckon the drought last summer burned your father's corn.

ADA. Yes, and a wolf killed Daisy, our cow. Then my little brother took sick and couldn't live any longer. My mother has never been the same since.

JOHNNIE. The wilderness likes to test folks. What do they call you?

ADA. Ada.

JOHNNIE. You're about ten years old, aren't you, Ada?

ADA. Ten today, but of course birthdays don't count in the backwoods.

JOHNNIE. So that's the way of it! Your birthday! Now just a moment. I may have something here. I carry little things here in case of need. (*Looks in bag.*) Yes, here's what I have for girls on their tenth birthday. (*Takes out pink ribbon.*) It would look fine in your hair.

ADA. It's not really for me? (JOHNNIE *nods head.*) It's beautiful!

JOHNNIE. It's the color of apple blossoms. That's why I always choose pink. There's something else I'd like to give you. It's the finest present in the world. (*Takes out small bag of deerskin.*) This is my treasure. And the most wonderful thing about it is that every year it will give more gifts.

ADA. What is it?

JOHNNIE. Want to see? (*Opens bag.*)

ADA. A seed!

JOHNNIE. An apple seed.

ADA. But why do you carry apple seeds around with you? We threw them away back home.

JOHNNIE. There were plenty of orchards around Boston.

ADA. Yes.

(MRS. BARTLETT *enters with wooden buckets.*)

JOHNNIE. Don't fear, ma'am. It's only me. I hear you are new settlers.

MRS. BARTLETT. We've been here more than a year. Are you going far?

JOHNNIE. Yes, I'm aiming to go into Illinois country, maybe as far west as the Mississippi.

MRS. BARTLETT. You're not settling here? You're just traveling through the wilderness for — for pleasure?

JOHNNIE. I like the wilderness — always have loved the woods. But now, of course, I've got my work. (*Shows her bag.*) I'm spreading orchards. I'm spreading apple trees through this frontier land.

MRS. BARTLETT. Oh! Then of course I know who you are! You're Johnnie Appleseed. (*Sits down.*)

JOHNNIE. That's what folks call me.

MRS. BARTLETT. Everyone knows about you. I've heard lots of tales. Some folks say you are a saint and some say —

JOHNNIE. I'm a fool.

MRS. BARTLETT. They all agree you've done great good. You were the hero of Fort Mansfield years back. You've often saved the settlers from Indian massacres.

JOHNNIE. I don't want anyone hurt. The Indians are my friends, too. I've lived in their wigwams.

NED (*enters shouting*). Sorry, Ma! I forgot to get the water. I'll carry the buckets. For the love of jumping Jonah, who are you?

JOHNNIE. I'm Jonathan Chapman, but folks call me Johnnie Appleseed.

NED. Johnnie Appleseed!

ADA. He's not afraid of Indians. He's lived with them.

NED. How many have you killed?

JOHNNIE. Not one. I'm not a killer.

MRS. BARTLETT. He's the man who saved Fort Mansfield years back, son. He was the only man who dared to set out through the woods to fetch reinforcements from thirty miles away.

JOHNNIE. Anyone would have done the same if he'd known the trails like me. I've helped the white men, and I've helped the Indians, too. I'm proud of that. I'm sorry to say there are some settlers who won't lift a finger for an Indian.

NED. Why should they? The savages would scalp us quick enough.

JOHNNIE. They haven't scalped me. The white man often starts the trouble. I couldn't sleep nights if I'd cheated the Indians out of their lands and hounded them from these parts the way white settlers have.

NED. Well, what else do you do besides help the Indians?

JOHNNIE. I follow the frontier, spreading orchards. Everywhere I go, I carry seeds to start orchards in the wilderness.

NED. But what do you get out of it? Folks won't pay for apple seeds.

JOHNNIE. I get along. Folks pay me what they can. If they haven't money, they sometimes give me cornmeal or clothes. Trouble is, I always meet up with someone who needs the clothes more than I do.

NED. Who wants an orchard in the backwoods anyhow?

JOHNNIE. Do you remember large, red-cheeked, juicy apples?

ADA. Oh, I want one!

JOHNNIE. An apple would taste mighty good right now, wouldn't it? Do you like roasted apples on a winter evening? Or maybe you would prefer a mug of cider in the fall, or a deep-dish apple pie.

NED. Oh, stop! Ma, do you remember the pies you used to make?

JOHNNIE. Maybe you would like an orchard by your house. How would it be to look out in the spring on an orchard in bloom? It's the most beautiful sight God ever made. You could have it right here.

MRS. BARTLETT. It sounds almost like heaven. (*Smiles and stands.*) You'll stay for dinner. We won't have apple pie, but you're welcome to share what there is.

JOHNNIE. I'll be proud to share. And maybe we can start an orchard as — well — as a sort of birthday gift for this little girl.

(From *Appleseed Farm*, by Emily Taft Douglas. Abingdon Press, Publishers.)

LEGEND OF THE CHRISTMAS ROSE
Characters

JOEL, a boy   FIRST KING

AMOS, a younger boy   SECOND KING

                                 THIRD KING

SCENE: *A hillside outside Bethlehem.* AMOS *sits center stage, crying.* JOEL *stands to the right of him. Leaves are scattered around the stage. Between the boys is a small pile of leaves, under which grows a Christmas rose.*

JOEL (*putting hand on* AMOS'S *shoulder trying to comfort him*). Come, Amos, do not cry.

AMOS. But I wanted to go. I wanted to go to Bethlehem to see the newborn Babe.

JOEL. The older men have gone. They will return and tell us what they saw.

AMOS. I wanted to go myself and see the Babe.

JOEL. You saw the angels. You heard them sing: "Glory to God in the highest, and on earth peace, good will toward men."

AMOS. Yes, I saw the angels. Now I want to see the Babe. I want to take him a gift. But I have no gift. (*Cries very hard.*)

JOEL. Don't you understand? Life is like that in these hills. Some people go. Some people stay. Some folks have gifts. Some folks have none. You and I, we have no gifts. So here we stay to watch the flock.

82

Amos. But I still want to see the Babe.

(*Sound of hoofs heard off stage.*)

Joel. What is that?

(*The* Three Kings *enter left, pantomiming to each other, not noticing* Joel *and* Amos. Joel *steps back, amazed, when he sees the fine robes.* Amos *pays no attention to them.*)

First King. The star? What has become of it? A cloud has covered it.

Second King. Shall we continue on this road? Does it lead to anywhere?

Third King. There are two boys. Let's question them. (*Advances toward* Joel.) Excuse me, lad, can you tell us where the newborn king may be?

Joel. Newborn king? Herod is king. He is not newborn, but you'll find him in Jerusalem. You are heading the wrong way.

Second King. No, no, not Herod. A ruler with a guiding star.

Joel. Caesar is ruler.

Third King. Let me explain a little more. We have come to worship a newborn king, a savior of the Jews, a savior of mankind.

Joel. A savior! He is the one of whom the angels sang — a Savior who is Christ the Lord.

Three Kings. That must be he.

Joel. You will find him in a manger, wrapped in swaddling clothes, the angels said. In the City of David. That is Bethlehem. This is the road that leads to Bethlehem.

First King. There! The star appears again! We shall follow it.

Second King. In a minute. Before we go, I'd like to ask a question. Why are you two small boys left alone in these lonely hills to guard the sheep?

Joel. Oh, sir, the older shepherds have gone to Bethlehem to bear gifts to the Babe. We had no gifts. (Amos *begins to weep harder.*)

Second King. We, too, bear gifts — gold, frankincense, and myrrh.

JOEL. Surely those are gifts worthy of a king!

SECOND KING. Come, do not feel so sad. A king who is also Christ the Lord will welcome gifts of any size if such gifts are offered with devotion, purity of heart, and love. Here, take these coins! Go see the Babe when the men return. (*Offers coins.*)

AMOS. No, no! They are not gifts from us. We have no gifts to give the Babe.

JOEL. Excuse his crying, sirs. A son of Old Judea should not weep. But this small boy has so great a wish to see the Babe. (*He kneels next to* AMOS.) Do not cry, Amos. Look. Your tears are falling on the ground. I'll wipe them away.

AMOS (*looking down*). Look! Look! (*The rose shines among the leaves. He picks it up.*) A rose! A pure white rose! (*He stands.*)

FIRST KING. A rose on barren soil this time of year! A miracle!

SECOND KING. A miracle, indeed! God's miracle! The boy's tears have become a rose.

THIRD KING. A rose fit for a king.

AMOS. Fit for a king? You really think so, sir?

THIRD KING. Indeed I do! It is a rose of unequalled beauty, a rose of miracles, a Christmas rose.

AMOS. A Christmas rose. A rose for Christ. When the men return, we shall take this rose to the Babe. (JOEL *and* AMOS *stand close together, very happy.*)

Pageants

A PAGEANT is a theatrical exhibition in which many people take part. Sometimes a pageant tells the story of the growth of a city or country. Sometimes it explains the work of a great organization, like the Boy Scouts or Girl Scouts. Sometimes a pageant is an elaboration of a legend.

Every year the Christmas story from the Bible is presented in hundreds of pageants. *Why the Chimes Rang,* by Raymond MacDonald Alden, *The Littlest Angel,* by Charles Tazewell, and "The Christmas Apple" from *This Way to Christmas,* by Ruth Sawyer, make beautiful pageants.

You can use pageants given here. Or you can write your own pageants, based on stories or history that you know.

THE WANDERING CHRIST CHILD
Characters

MOTHER	LITTLE ANGEL CHOIR
GRETA	CHERUBIM, young angels
KARL	SERAPHIM, larger angels
CHILD	ARCHANGEL

SCENE: *A cottage on Christmas Eve. The setting and clothing may be old-fashioned, but they need not represent any particular period or country. There are no stockings, no tree, nor any other suggestion of the Christmas season. Left stage is an open fireplace with a log in it. An electric light, turned on to resemble a burning fire, is back of log. At left is a small pile of logs. KARL sits on a small stool near the logs, whittling. He wears sock-like slippers. GRETA sits in an armchair or rocker at right of fireplace, as far downstage as possible, knitting. She has shawl around her shoulders.*

Back center stage is an old chest containing two blankets. Right stage is a small dining table, with tureen and soup ladle and bowls in center. On one corner is a huge old family Bible. MOTHER *is dusting. She, too, wears a shawl.*

There must be an outside entrance, right, and a house entrance, center, if possible. If the stage does not have a curtain, characters may enter through house door to go to their places.

Off stage, strains of "Silent Night" are heard.

GRETA. Oh, Mother, listen to the trumpets in the village. Hear the choir singing, "Silent Night, Holy Night."

MOTHER. Yes, child, I hear.

GRETA. Isn't it beautiful, Mother? Very beautiful?

MOTHER. Indeed it is beautiful.

GRETA. It's so calm and peaceful. It gives me a feeling.

KARL. A feeling? What kind of feeling, Greta?

GRETA. I don't know. Just a feeling. (*Puts knitting on table. Rises and crosses to center. Stops.*) A Christmas feeling.

MOTHER (*putting aside duster*). There, not a speck of dust remains. (*Crosses room.*) If the Christ Child visits our home this Christmas Eve, he will find it spick-and-span. (*Sits in chair near fire.*)

GRETA. Do you really think he visits the earth each year?

MOTHER. Who knows? It's an old legend, a German legend, that he comes to earth each year, bringing peace and joy wherever he walks. But enough of legends. Bring me the Good Book, Greta. Let us hear the word as it is written. (GRETA *crosses room to get Bible.*) And, Karl, throw another log on the fire.

KARL. Gladly, Mother. (*Rises and lays log on fire.*)

MOTHER. The wind blows cold and wild tonight. God help the poor traveler who must walk about. (GRETA *hands* MOTHER *the Bible.*) Thank you, Greta. Draw up your stool, Karl. (*He places stool at her feet.* GRETA *stands behind* MOTHER's *chair, looking over her shoulder.* MOTHER *opens Bible.*) Now let's see. Luke, the second chapter.

GRETA. Start with the shepherds, Mother, and the angels. I like the angels. (*She points to place.*)

MOTHER. "And there were in the same country shepherds abiding in the field, keeping watch over their flock by night. And, lo, the angel of the Lord came upon them, and the glory of the Lord shone round about them: and they were sore afraid. And the angel said unto them, Fear not: for, behold, I bring you good tidings of great joy, which shall be to all people. For unto you is born this day in the city of David a Saviour, which is Christ the Lord." (*Knocking off stage.*)

KARL. Listen, Mother, what is that? A knock?

MOTHER. No, no. Only the wind blowing a branch across the door. Now —

GRETA (*pointing*). You're here, Mother.

MOTHER. Oh, yes. "And this shall be a sign unto you; Ye shall find the babe wrapped in swaddling clothes, lying in a manger."

(*Knock is again heard.*)

KARL. I hear it again, Mother. I am sure it is a knock. I must see. (*Goes to door. Sees* CHILD *standing outside. He is cold, shivering.*) Mother, come. (KARL *leads* CHILD *into room.* CHILD *looks around, bewildered. He doesn't speak.* MOTHER *rises. Looks at* CHILD. *Goes to almost center stage.*)

MOTHER. Child, child. (*Kneels, extending her arms.*) Come here. (CHILD *comes to* MOTHER'S *arms. She puts her arms around him.*) You are shivering. Freezing. Here, take my shawl. (*Wraps shawl around* CHILD'S *shoulders.*) Sit by the fire. (*Helps him into big chair. Goes to table, ladles soup from large bowl to smaller one.*)

GRETA. Wrap mine around your knees. (*She covers* CHILD'S *knees with her shawl.*)

KARL. Your feet are freezing. Take my slippers. (*Removes his slippers and puts them on* CHILD'S *feet.*)

MOTHER. The broth is still hot. Drink some. (*She hands* CHILD *bowl. He drinks. Hands bowl to* GRETA. *She takes it back to table.*) Where did you come from, child? Why are you alone?

KARL. I'll see if anyone is near. (*Goes to door.*) I can't see anyone. Mother, shall I go and search?

MOTHER. No, Karl. You might get lost. We shall keep the fire burning bright. It will guide any wanderer to our home, and also keep the child warm.

GRETA (*crossing to almost center stage*). Look, Mother, the child has fallen asleep. (*She lifts lid of chest and takes out blanket.*)

MOTHER. So he has, poor dear.

GRETA. I am gong to sleep by the fire. If he cries, I shall hear him. (*Curls up in blanket in front of fire.*)

KARL (*getting second blanket*). I, too, shall sleep here. (*Rolls up.*)

MOTHER. Good night, children. Call me if you need me. (*Exits.*)

(*Music off stage. "All This Night Rejoices."* CHILD *rises. Folds shawls and lays them on chair. Takes off slippers. Puts them on chair. Goes to* GRETA, *raising hand in blessing. Goes to* KARL, *again raising hand in blessing. Goes to door where* MOTHER *went out. Raises hand in blessing. Exits by outside door.*)

(LITTLE ANGEL CHOIR *comes down aisle and goes up on stage as music changes to "What Child Is This?" They look at sleeping children and sing "Away in a Manger."*)

(KARL *and* GRETA *stand as the* ANGELS *sing.* MOTHER *enters and watches. All are puzzled.* LITTLE ANGEL CHOIR *leaves as* CHERUBIM *enter.*)

(CHERUBIM *sing "It Came Upon a Midnight Clear."*)

(SERAPHIM *enter, join* CHERUBIM *in singing "Hark the Herald Angels Sing."*)

(MOTHER, GRETA, *and* KARL *have moved up in front of angels.*)

MOTHER. Greta? Karl? Where is the child?

GRETA. I don't know.

KARL. He's gone.

ARCHANGEL (*stepping forward*). No, he is not gone. He abides with you forever.

MOTHER, GRETA, KARL. Forever?

ARCHANGEL. The child you sheltered here tonight was the Christ Child, wandering through the world to bring peace and happiness to the hearts of all. He was cold, and you took him in. He was hungry and you gave him food. He was tired and you gave him rest. His blessing rests upon this house forever.

(*All* ANGELS, MOTHER, GRETA, KARL *sing "Joy to the World."* ANGELS *leave on last verse.*)

MOTHER (*standing center stage with an arm around each child*). May the peace of God which passeth all understanding keep your hearts and minds. Amen.

GRETA and KARL. Amen. (*Look up at* MOTHER *and smile.*)

(*If there is a curtain, it is pulled. If there is no curtain,* MOTHER *and children turn. They exit through house door,* MOTHER *first, then* GRETA, *then* KARL.)

YOUR COUNTRY AND MINE
Characters

READER	MIDWESTERN FARMERS
CHORUS	HILLBILLY SINGERS
NEW ENGLAND WORKERS	COWBOYS
VIRGINIAN DANCERS	WESTERN MOUNTAIN SETTLERS
SPANISH-AMERICAN DANCERS	

READER *stands on one side of the stage.* CHORUS *stands in front of the audience, to the left.* CHORUS *joins in singing all songs.*

(CHORUS *sings first verse of "America the Beautiful."*)

READER. "From sea to shining sea," the United States of America stands today — one nation, one people, united. The United States is a big nation, an interesting nation, alive and alert because she is composed of many individuals, each with his own background, each with his own way of thinking.

(CHORUS *sings second verse of "America the Beautiful."*)

READER. The early settlers who came to New England were a sturdy lot. They found rocky soil for their crops, a cruel sea for fishing, and long bitter winters. They were a resourceful people, determined to make the best of any situation. They were religious people and hard workers.

(NEW ENGLAND WORKERS, *wearing cotton clothes, enter left, singing "Work for the Night Is Coming." After song, they exit left.*)

90

READER. In the southeastern states the climate is mild and the soil fertile. Early settlers built large plantations and enjoyed luxurious and gracious living.

(VIRGINIAN DANCERS, *wearing party clothes, enter right, singing "Carry Me Back to Old Virginny." Dance Virginia reel. Exit right.*)

READER. The Spanish settled the far Southwest. With them came a love of color and gay music. At fiesta time all work stopped while boys and girls, men and women, sang and danced.

(SPANISH-AMERICAN DANCERS *enter left, singing "La Cucaracha." Girls wear full, brightly colored skirts. Boys wear sashes. Two or three couples dance a rumba. All exit left.*)

READER. The fertile soil of the Midwest attracted farmers, who worked hard from dawn until dark. Often during the long and lazy summer evenings they would sit around and spin a tale or take a stroll down to the old mill stream.

(MIDWESTERN FARMERS *enter right, singing "Down by the Old Mill Stream." Girls wear simple cotton dresses. Boys wear dungarees. After song they exit right.*)

READER. Life in the Appalachian Mountains was rugged. So rugged that some folk wondered why they should try to get ahead. Instead they would take down the fiddle and sing and dance.

(HILLBILLY SINGERS, *wearing cotton clothes, enter left, singing "She'll Be Comin' Round the Mountain When She Comes." They add motions and comments at the end of each of the many verses. "She'll be drivin' six white horses when she comes. Giddy-up!" "We'll all go out to meet her when she comes. Hi, Babe!" "We'll kill the old red rooster when she comes. Hack! Hack!" "She'll be wearing long red flannels when she comes. Scratch! Scratch!" etc. After song, all exit left.*)

READER. In the western plains country cowboys often led a lonely life. For company, they sang songs all their own.

(COWBOYS *enter right, singing "Whoopee, Ti-Yi-Yo." Exit right.*)

READER. The mountains of the West with their fertile valleys beckoned many settlers. Here the newcomers found peace and joy and prosperity in their little gray homes in the West.

(WESTERN MOUNTAIN SETTLERS *enter left, singing "My Little Gray Home in the West." Exit left.*)

READER. Truly each section of the United States has its own history, its own folklore, its own songs. Yet, from East to West, from North to South, she stands one nation, united. Her people everywhere unite to bless her name. God bless the United States of America — your country and mine!

(*Half of the actors enter from the left, half from the right. They march in drill formation which mixes them completely so that a worker from New England will be standing near a Spanish-American dancer, etc.*)

(ALL *sing "God Bless America."*)

II. Puppets Are the Actors

THE SECOND part of this book is about puppets. When you play with puppets, you have to do two things at once. You have to work the puppets, and you have to do the talking, too. It's not hard, and it's fun.

A puppet is really a doll, shaped more or less like a human being, an animal, or an imaginary creature. There are many different kinds of puppets, ranging from very simple to very complicated ones.

You can have your puppets sing together, tell each other jokes and jingles, or act little plays. Make up your own plays or use those suggested for each type of puppet. Some plays are suitable for all types of puppets. Some of the pantomime plays (pages 26-37) can be used for puppets if you add words. So can some of the plays (pages 67-84).

If you are using more than one puppet, be sure to use a different voice for each, according to the character each represents. Puppets usually wiggle when they speak so that the audience can tell which is talking.

Play with your puppets. Then put on puppet acts and plays for your family and friends. Have fun as you *act it out* with puppets.

Fist Puppets

MAKE A FACE on the back of your hand. Draw it or cut out construction-paper features and paste them in place. Clench your fist. Tie a handkerchief around the face for a bonnet, if you like. Make a face on the back of your other hand. Hold the faces to the audience. Let the puppets sing a song, like "Billy Boy" (page 96). One puppet asks the questions, the other gives the answers. Or let the puppets say a jingle or act out a joke.

WHAT'S YOUR NAME?

One puppet asks the questions; the other gives the answers as they say this old jingle.

QUESTION. What's your name?
ANSWER. Puddin' tame.
QUESTION. What's your other?
ANSWER. Bread and butter.
QUESTION. Where do you live?
ANSWER. In a sieve.
QUESTION. What's your number?
ANSWER. Cucumber.

BILLY BOY

Sing "Billy Boy," having one puppet ask the questions and the other give the answers.

Oh, where have you been, Billy Boy, Billy Boy?
Oh, where have you been, charming Billy?

I have been to seek a wife,
She's the joy of my life;
But she's a young thing and cannot leave her mother.

Can she make a pumpkin pie, Billy Boy, Billy Boy?
Can she make a pumpkin pie, charming Billy?

Yes, she can make a pumpkin pie
Quick as a cat can wink its eye;
But she's a young thing and cannot leave her mother.

Oh, how old is she, Billy Boy, Billy Boy?
Oh, how old is she, charming Billy?

Twice six, twice seven,
Twice twenty and eleven;
Isn't she the young thing who cannot leave her mother!

I WANT A —
Characters
MOTHER   JANIE

MOTHER. I want you to go to the general store for me, Janie.
JANIE. All right, Mother.
MOTHER. I'll make a list of things for you to get.
JANIE. Don't make a list, Mother. I'll remember everything.

96

MOTHER. Are you sure?

JANIE. Positive.

MOTHER. Well — I want a pound of butter,
   A spool of white thread,
   A dozen ripe oranges,
   And a loaf of bread.

JANIE. All right, Mother.
   I want a pound of butter,
   A spool of white thread,
   A dozen ripe oranges,
   And a loaf of bread.

MOTHER. That's right. Good-by, Janie. (*Exits.*)

JANIE. Good-by, Mother. (*Hops up and down. Hums.*) Now let's see.
   I want a loaf of butter,
   A spool of white bread,
   A pound of ripe oranges,
   And a dozen thread.

Something sounds wrong. I know.
   I want a dozen butter,
   And a pound of bread,
   A spool of ripe oranges,
   And a loaf of thread.

That doesn't sound right either. Mother, what did you tell me to get? I think I need a list. I want a dozen spools of butter — No! Mother, what do I want?

WHICH WAY?
Characters
SPEAKER   LITTLE BOY

SPEAKER. Excuse me, son, do you know where the high school is?
I have to make a speech there in half an hour.

LITTLE BOY. Sure, I know where the high school is. Let's see. You
know where Swanson's Bakery is?

SPEAKER. I'm sorry. I don't know where Swanson's Bakery is.

LITTLE BOY. Well, you know where the post office is?

SPEAKER. No, I'm sorry. I don't know where the post office is.

LITTLE BOY. Well, you know where the First Methodist Church is?

SPEAKER. No. I don't know where the First Methodist Church is.

LITTLE BOY. I'm sorry, mister. You don't know enough for me to
start to tell you where the high school is.

Ring Puppets

A RING PUPPET is a picture of a character pasted on a paper ring that fits your finger. Wear the puppet with its head toward your wrist. Make the puppet walk. Make puppets for other fingers. Let them dance together or put on little plays.

IMPERSONATIONS

Make ring puppets which resemble nursery-rhyme or storybook characters. See if you can talk the way you think they would speak and do it so well that another person can guess whom you are impersonating.

Try to impersonate people you know, or people in the news.

How do you think people who lived long ago talked? Say something you think the historic character might have said. Can your friends guess the person you have in mind? Let them ask questions until they guess correctly.

FIVE LITTLE RABBITS

Make five ring puppets for the five little rabbits. Put them on the thumb and fingers of your right hand. As each rabbit speaks, you make that puppet bob up and down. The first puppet is on the thumb; the second one, on the pointer finger; the two little ones, on the ring finger and little finger; the big one, on the middle finger. When you say "Bang!" slap the table hard with the palm of your left hand.

Five little rabbits went out to walk.
They liked to boast as well as talk.
The first one said, "I hear a gun!"
The second one said, "I will not run!"
Two little ones said, "Let's sit in the shade."
The big one said, "I'm not afraid!"
Bang, bang! went the gun.
See the five little rabbits run!

GRASSHOPPER AND ANTS
Characters

GRASSHOPPER   FIVE ANTS

Make a GRASSHOPPER *ring puppet for the middle finger of your right hand. Make five* ANT *ring puppets, one for each finger and the thumb of your left hand. Use a table for the field. Put a piece of crumpled paper on the right-hand side of the table for an ant hill.*

SCENE: *A field.* ANTS *are busily crawling around the table, gathering food and taking it back to the ant hill.* GRASSHOPPER *is jumping up and down.*

100

GRASSHOPPER (*chanting and dancing*).
>Fiddle-de-dee! Strum, strum, strun!
>Summer is the time for fun.
>Fiddle-de-dee! Hey, hey, hey!
>Summer is the time for play.

You silly ants, what are you doing?

MIDDLE-FINGER ANT. Can't you see? We're getting food.

GRASSHOPPER. Getting food? How silly can you be? There's food all around you.

MIDDLE-FINGER ANT. Yes, there's food now. But wait till winter comes.

GRASSHOPPER. Wait? Why should I waste my life waiting? Come, dance with me.

>Fiddle-de-dee! Strum, strum, strun!
>Summer is the time for fun!

Come on, ants, dance with me.

>Fiddle-de-dee! Hey, hey, hey!
>Summer is the time for play.

Come on, ants, join me.

MIDDLE-FINGER ANT. First we work and then we play.

OTHER ANTS. Yes, first we work and then we play.

MIDDLE-FINGER ANT. Come on, ants. Very little time is left.

GRASSHOPPER. Listen! Fiddle-de-dee! Hey, hey, hey!

MIDDLE-FINGER ANT. Don't listen to that crazy, mixed-up grasshopper.

(ANTS *run busily around the table.*)

GRASSHOPPER. Who's crazy? Who's mixed up? Fiddle-de-dee! I feel a wind blowing. It's cold! Maybe the ants are right. I'd better get a house. (*Hops around.*) I can't get a house. There's too much wind. I'd better get some food. Oh, I'm cold! I'm hungry. It's snowing! What'll I do? Where'll I go? What'll I eat? I am going to die. (*Hops slowly.*)

ANTS (*behind hill, chanting*).
>Tra-la-la! Work is done.
>Now's the time we have our fun.

GRASSHOPPER. Say! I hear music. Someone is singing! How can any-one sing when it's so cold? I'm freezing. (*Goes to ant hill.*) Help! Help! I'm freezing. (*Drops near ant hill.*)

ANTS (*chanting*).

Tra-la-la! Work is done.

Now's the time we have our fun.

GRASSHOPPER (*faintly*). Help — help —

MIDDLE-FINGER ANT. I hear someone. Let's see who it is. (ANTS *come to* GRASSHOPPER.)

ANTS. It's Grasshopper.

POINTER-FINGER ANT. Foolish insect! Let him die! He played all summer while we worked. He deserves to die.

MIDDLE-FINGER ANT. No, we can't let him die. Let's drag him into the hill.

(ANTS *drag* GRASSHOPPER *to hill. They wait on him.*)

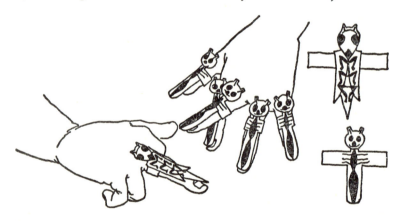

MIDDLE-FINGER ANT. Come, Grasshopper, sit near the fire.

THUMB ANT. Come, eat this hot food.

POINTER-FINGER ANT. Get your feet warm.

GRASSHOPPER (*slowly coming to*). Where am I? In an ant hill? How good I feel! I was freezing. I was starving. You saved me. I don't deserve all this.

MIDDLE-FINGER ANT. Maybe you're right. You don't deserve help. You played all summer while we worked.

GRASSHOPPER. Yet you are good to me. I don't deserve all this.

MIDDLE-FINGER ANT. I guess all of us get more good things than we deserve. You are no exception, Grasshopper.

GRASSHOPPER. Say! That calls for a song and dance. A new song — the one I heard when I was outside.

GRASSHOPPER and ANTS (*jumping up and down and chanting*).
        Tra-la-la! Work is done.
        Now's the time we have our fun.

Cardboard Puppets

A CARDBOARD PUPPET is a paper doll, pasted on cardboard. It has a handle, usually at the base of the doll. If you make several puppets, you and your friends can put on little plays.

You can act out nursery rhymes, like "Miss Muffet," "Jack Be Nimble," or "Mother Hubbard." You can act out fairy stories, legends, incidents from history, or everyday adventures.

If you are putting on a play for an audience, you can conceal yourself behind a sofa or a covered table. Or you can lay a card table on its side with the top facing the audience. Hold your puppet so that your hand does not show.

BABY-SITTING

Think of something that might happen to you and act it out with cardboard puppets. For example, MOTHER asks you to baby-sit while she goes to the hospital to see Grandma.

"But, Mom," you answer, "the kids are coming over to jump rope. Can't you go some other time?"

MOTHER explains that visiting hours are from two to four o'clock. It's after three and she has to rush. She says good-by.

BABY says, "By," then looks at you. You are sulking. BABY cries. You yell, "Why am I always stuck with you?"

BABY jumps up and down yelling.

KATE and SANDRA come to the door, asking you to come out to jump rope. You yell that you are baby-sitting. BABY leaves scene. You hear *crash!* You yell at BABY. Tell girls to come in. Go get BABY, scolding him.

You return with BABY. Girls think he is cute.

KATE says, "Jump!" She jumps up high, and so does BABY.

SANDRA says, "Hop!" She goes up just a little way. So does BABY.

KATE says, "Go bop, bop, bop." BABY leans forward in funny way three times. Everyone laughs.

Then you think of a new game. You say a verse and go through the motions.

> Jump! Jump! — Hop, hop, hop!
> Then lean forward, bop, bop, bop!
> Keep it up! Never stop!

Everyone joins in the game. Before you know it, MOTHER comes home. She thinks your game is wonderful. She gives you each a cookie and reminds you that there is still time for jumping rope.

As you and the girls go out, MOTHER and BABY are left alone. BABY shows MOTHER how to jump. Soon MOTHER and BABY are playing.

> Jump! Jump! — Hop, hop, hop!
> Then lean forward, bop, bop, bop!
> Keep it up! Never stop!

ANYONE COULD, BUT —
Characters

LORD CHAMBERLAIN   TWO PEASANT WOMEN

KING   TWO MERCHANTS

TWO SHEPHERDS   GREG

In addition to the characters you will need a property that looks like a stone, made of cardboard like the puppets.

SCENE: *A road. Stone is in the middle of the road.* LORD CHAMBERLAIN *and* KING *stand on either side of the stone.*

LORD CHAMBERLAIN. Your Highness, I do not understand. Why did you dig a hole in the road, put a pot of gold in the hole, and then put this huge stone above the gold? The stone is in the way.

KING. Yes, it is. But this stone may help me find a man.

LORD CHAMBERLAIN. Your Highness, you'll never catch a thief this way. He'll never look for gold down there.

KING. I'm not looking for a thief. I doubt if anyone will find gold down there. But someone may.

LORD CHAMBERLAIN. Your Highness, are you feeling well? Is your head all right?

KING. Never fear, Lord Chamberlain. My head is well. My heart is heavy. You see, I am worried about my people.

LORD CHAMBERLAIN. I can understand that. They bring you every little problem that they have.

KING. That's true.

LORD CHAMBERLAIN. They depend on you for everything.

KING. That's just the trouble. They depend upon me too much. I think they have forgotten how to help themselves. I think they have forgotten how to help one another.

LORD CHAMBERLAIN. But what good is a stone in the road?

KING. You'll see. *Shh!* Here come two shepherds returning from market. Let's hide. (*They exit.*)

106

FIRST SHEPHERD. Just look at that! A stone in the road!

SECOND SHEPHERD. Of all things! Thank goodness, it wasn't there this morning!

FIRST SHEPHERD. That's right. The sheep would have had to go around.

SECOND SHEPHERD. I hope someone tells the king about this before next market day.

FIRST SHEPHERD. I hope he gets it out of the way — and fast! (SHEPHERDS *exit complaining.* KING *and* LORD CHAMBERLAIN *appear.*)

KING. See what I mean?

LORD CHAMBERLAIN. I think so. *Shh!* Here come two peasant women. (LORD CHAMBERLAIN *and* KING *exit.* WOMEN *appear.*)

FIRST WOMAN. Well, a nice kettle of fish!

SECOND WOMAN. Not fish, sister. Not fish. But a mighty ugly stone in the road.

FIRST WOMAN. Glad it isn't dark. I might have stubbed my toe.

SECOND WOMAN. Might do worse than that. What is this world coming to. A stone in the road! Where is the king? (*Exit complaining.*)

FIRST MERCHANT (*entering with* SECOND MERCHANT). Yes, business was good, very good. But look! What is this? A stone in the road.

SECOND MERCHANT. It's an outrage! Something should be done at once.

FIRST MERCHANT. A stone like that will interfere with trade.

SECOND MERCHANT. I wonder if the authorities have been notified.

FIRST MERCHANT. The king must be slipping, allowing a stone to remain in the middle of the road. (MERCHANTS *exit complaining*.)

GREG (*entering whistling*). Wow! Look at that stone! Right in the middle of the road. Lucky I saw it before it got dark. Someone might have bumped into it and got hurt. Wonder if I can move it. Let's see. If I push here, it will roll down there. Nothing's in the way. (*Pushes stone.*) There! (*Stone disappears.*) There she rolls. (*Looks down. Gasps.*) Hey! What's in the hole? Gold! It must be the king's gold. No one else has that much gold! Wonder if someone stole it. I must tell the king. What shall I do? I can't carry it all. I must get help.

KING (*appearing*). Wait, lad. I've been looking for you.

GREG. Oh, your Highness, I just found this gold. I didn't steal it, sir. Honest, I didn't. There was a stone here. I rolled it away. Believe me, sir!

KING. I believe you, lad, because I saw it all. I planned it all.

GREG. You planned it all?

KING. Yes, I have been looking for someone in my land who thinks of others, for someone who can do things for himself. I waited all day, lad. But at last I found you.

GREG. All day, sir? Why, anyone could move that stone.

KING. Anyone could do it, but only you did do it. God bless you, lad. The gold is yours.

Blockhead Puppets

A BLOCKHEAD PUPPET has a funny head on a stick. Nail a small piece of scrap lumber onto a piece of lath. You can make a funny head out of any shape. Or wad cotton or cloth into the shape of a head. Cover it with crepe paper or cloth. Insert a stick into the middle of the wad. Wind a rubber band around the bottom of the head to hold

the covering in place. Paint features on the head, or cut out construction-paper features and paste them in place. Or you can combine the two, painting the eyes and lips, and pasting on the ears, nose, and eyebrows.

You can also use a big spoon for a blockhead puppet. Cut out construction-paper features. Scotch-tape them in place on the back of the

spoon. For a hat, Scotch-tape a paper baking cup in place. Make crepe-paper clothes.

Get behind a sofa or covered table. Hold the blockhead puppets so that the audience can see the heads. Wiggle each puppet when it speaks. Make up plays about trips through space, imaginary characters, or regular people. Or act out stories that you know.

109

THE THREE WISHES
Characters

OLD MAN   OLD WOMAN

In addition to the characters you will need a table covered with a cloth, set with dishes and dinner on it. Make it of cardboard and nail it onto a piece of lath. Make a paper sausage with a little piece of Scotch tape coming out over the end.

SCENE: *Kitchen.* OLD WOMAN *is alone.*

OLD WOMAN. Work, work, work! All I do is work. All I do is keep house and feed Old Man. Nothing exciting ever happens around here. Just work, work, work!

OLD MAN (*entering*). Old Woman! Old Woman! I have news for you.

OLD WOMAN. News, indeed! What kind of news can you have?

OLD MAN. When I was in the woods, I met a fairy.

OLD WOMAN. A fairy? Now that's a fine story!

OLD MAN. Yes, I met a fairy when I started to cut down a tree.

OLD WOMAN. You met a fairy when you started to cut down a tree? You cut down trees every day and you don't meet fairies.

OLD MAN. This was a special tree. The fairy came out of the tree. She took my hand. (OLD WOMAN *bobs up and down.*) Now don't get excited. The fairy said, "Don't cut down that tree." "What will you give me?" I asked. "I'll give you three wishes," she said. "All right," said I. "But mind," said she, "the next three wishes you make will come true."

OLD WOMAN. Three wishes, indeed! I don't believe a word of it.

OLD MAN. You don't believe it? All right, I'll show you. I wish I had a table all set with dinner in front of me right now.

(*Table appears.*)

OLD MAN. See?

OLD WOMAN. Yes, I see. But you've used up one of your wishes. You good-for-nothing blockhead! You've used up one of your wishes! You could have wished for a new house, or for fine clothes. Look at these rags! You could have wished for a carriage. You could have wished for a maid to help with the housework. You could have —

OLD MAN (*bobbing up and down*). Be quiet! I say be quiet!

OLD WOMAN. I won't be quiet. Day after day I work, work, work. Never get ahead! Now you have a wish. What do you wish for? A table set with food!

OLD MAN. I'm glad I wished for that table set with food. What's more, I wish a sausage was stuck onto the end of your nose.

OLD WOMAN (*disappearing*). What? Oh-oh-oh — (*Keeps up her cries while you stick the paper sausage to her nose.*)

OLD MAN. Where are you? Good wife, where did you go?

OLD WOMAN (*reappearing*). Here I am. Boo, hoo, hoo! Look what happened to me!

OLD MAN. Why, that's a sausage on your nose! How did it get there?

OLD WOMAN. You had a wish. You wished that a sausage would go on the end of my nose. Here it is. Boo, hoo, hoo!

OLD MAN. There, there, don't cry. You'll get used to having a sausage on your nose.

OLD WOMAN. What? A sausage on my nose, all my life? No, no, no!

111

OLD MAN. It's too bad. But what can I do about it?

OLD WOMAN. What can you do? You can wish to get this sausage off my nose!

OLD MAN. But I have only one more wish. There are lots of things I ought to wish for. You mentioned money, clothes, house —

OLD WOMAN. What good are money, clothes, house if I have a sausage on my nose? Boo, hoo, hoo!

OLD MAN. There, there, don't cry. I hate to see you cry.

OLD WOMAN. Do you like to see a sausage on my nose?

OLD MAN. No.

OLD WOMAN. Then, please, please, wish to get it off.

OLD MAN. Well —

OLD WOMAN. I'll keep the house neat and clean.

OLD MAN. Well —

OLD WOMAN. I'll cook good meals.

OLD MAN. Well —

OLD WOMAN. I'll love you truly all my life.

OLD MAN. Then I wish the sausage to come off your nose. (*He hums.* OLD WOMAN *disappears. Pull sausage off her nose. She reappears.*)

BOTH (*putting heads together*). Now we'll live happily ever after.

Bag-Head Puppets

THE BAG-HEAD PUPPET, like the blockhead puppet, shows only the head when it acts. To make a bag-head puppet, stuff a paper bag loosely with newspaper. Leave room at the bottom for tying. Put a sturdy stick or a piece of lath, about a foot longer than the bag, well into the stuffing, rearranging the paper if necessary. Tie the bottom of the bag around the stick.

You can paint features, or you can paste on features cut from con-

struction paper, or combine the two. Use strips of construction paper or crepe paper for hair. Add a collar, or even clothes, if you like.

If you want to put on a play, make several bag-head puppets. Get behind a covered table, sofa, or bookcase. Hold the sticks up so that only the puppets' heads show.

If you need properties in the play, draw pictures on heavy paper and cut them out. They should be large. Tack each picture to a piece of lath. Be careful not to turn this property during the play.

You can make up a play about funny bag-head-puppet people or you can have the puppets act out an old fairy tale or legend.

GOLD, RUBIES, OR SALT?

Characters

KING BIGHEAD   PRINCESS SALLY

PRINCESS GOLDIE   COOK

PRINCESS RUBY   KING PLEASE-'EM

In addition to the characters, you will need a ring and a large dish of food, made of heavy paper and mounted on sticks.

ACT I

SCENE: *Throne room of* KING BIGHEAD. KING BIGHEAD *is on stage.* PRINCESSES GOLDIE, RUBY, *and* SALLY *enter. All wear crowns.*

KING BIGHEAD. Good morning! Good morning! How are my daughters today? How are the princesses of the realm of Bighead?

PRINCESSES (*together, bobbing up and down*). Fine, thank you, Father Bighead. Fine, your Highness.

KING BIGHEAD. This morning I have a question which I should like to ask each of you.

PRINCESSES (*together*). Oh, good! We like questions.

SALLY. Is this question a riddle?

KING BIGHEAD. No, this isn't a riddle. This is a very serious question.

PRINCESSES. Oh-oh-oh —

114

KING BIGHEAD. I am ruler of the realm of Bighead.

PRINCESS. Oh, yes, Father! We know you are King Bighead, ruler of the realm of Bighead.

KING BIGHEAD. Now as King Bighead, ruler of the realm of Bighead, it is very important for me to know whether or not my daughters love me.

PRINCESSES. Oh, yes, we love you. We all love you.

KING BIGHEAD. But I want to know how much you love me.

PRINCESSES. Oh, lots and lots! We love you very much.

KING BIGHEAD. Stop and think. Then each of you answer in turn. Goldie, how much do you love your father?

GOLDIE. Father, I love you as much as you love gold.

KING BIGHEAD. Good! Good! I named you Goldie so that you would remember to love me as much as I love gold.

(GOLDIE *goes to the end of the line of princesses.* RUBY *stands next to her father.*)

KING BIGHEAD. Now, Ruby, how much do you love me?

RUBY. Father, I love you as much as you love rubies.

KING BIGHEAD. Good! Good! That is why I named you Ruby so that you would remember to love me as much as I love rubies.

(RUBY *goes to the end of the line of princesses.* SALLY *stands next to her father.*)

KING BIGHEAD. Now, my last and most beloved daughter, Sally. Tell me, how much do you love me?

SALLY. Father, I love you as much as you love salt.

KING BIGHEAD (*in rage*). Salt? Plain, common, everyday salt? Come now, Sally, you must be joking. Do not make a game with your poor old father.

SALLY. Indeed, I am not joking, Father. My sisters have told you that they love you as much as you love rubies and gold. I tell you truly, I love you as much as you love salt.

KING BIGHEAD. Salt? Every man in the street, every peasant in the fields, even the beasts in the woods have salt. Yet you say that you love me as much as I love salt.

SALLY. I do love you, Father. I'm trying to tell you how much.

KING BIGHEAD. To think that my daughter says she loves me as much as I love salt! Sally, you are ungrateful, insulting, disrespectful! Be gone! Be gone! Out of my sight!

SALLY (*sobbing*). No, no! Believe me! I love you!

GOLDIE and RUBY (*crying*). No, no! No, Father!

KING BIGHEAD. Be gone, I say! Never set foot in my realm again.

SALLY. Oh, Father, some day you'll understand. (*Turns and goes sadly away.*)

KING BIGHEAD. My baby, gone for good! At least I have two loving daughters.

GOLDIE and RUBY. Yes, Father.

ACT II

SCENE: *Kitchen of* KING PLEASE-'EM. SALLY *and* COOK *are preparing dinner.* SALLY *no longer wears a crown.*

SALLY. Please, Cook, please let me make the main dish for the royal dinner.

COOK. No! No! His Highness, King Please-'Em, has an important guest today. It is his Highness, King Bighead, ruler of the realm of Bighead, no less!

SALLY. Please, Cook. I once lived in the realm of Bighead. I know exactly what his Highness likes, and I know how to cook it.

COOK. You lived in the realm of Bighead? You know what his Highness likes? Then why are you here?

SALLY. Cook, you promised not to ask questions if I served you well.

COOK (*nodding*). Yes.

SALLY. I have served you well, haven't I? I've washed the pans, scrubbed the floor, peeled potatoes.

Cook. Yes.

Sally. Then please, please, let me make the favorite dish of King Bighead.

Cook. All right, go ahead. But mind, season it to his taste. I'll have the boy get more wood so that you can cook it well. (*Exits.*)

Sally. I'll season it to his taste. If I remember correctly, he likes rubies and gold. But he doesn't care much for salt.

ACT III

Scene: *Dining room of* King Please-'Em. *On the table before* King Please-'Em *and* King Bighead *is a large dish of food.*

King Please-'Em. Ah, how glad I am to have you here, dining with me! You know I, King Please-'Em, like to please everyone. A little secret though. (Kings *put heads together.*) I would rather please a king than common people.

King Bighead. Ha! Ha! Ha! That's good! When kings try to please me, King Bighead, my head gets bigger. Ha! Ha! Ha!

King Please-'Em. Very good! Both of us are happy! Let us eat. Well, what is this? It looks like a new dish to me.

King Bighead. I do believe it is turtle-rabbit-wasps'-nest jumble. My favorite dish! Nothing could please me more. To think that you learned my favorite dish and had your cook prepare it! *Mmmmm —*

King Please-'Em. Well, I'm glad you like it. I'm delighted. I like to please you. Pray begin to eat.

King Bighead (*leaning over to take a bite, then jerking back*). Something's wrong! This is terrible, horrible, insipid, tasteless, disagreeable, shameful —

King Please-'Em (*leaning forward as* King Bighead *speaks*). Wait a minute. I'd just say it tastes bad. Cook! Cook! Cook!

Cook (*entering*). Yes, your Highness! Yes, your Highness! Something wrong, your Highness?

King Please-'Em. Something wrong? Nothing right! I am displeased with this dish.

Cook (shaking). Oh-oh-oh —

King Please-Em. When I am displeased, someone loses his head.

Cook (*trembling*). Oh, sir! It was the little maid who helps me. She said she used to live in the realm of Bighead. She said she knew what King Bighead liked. Oh-oh-oh —

King Please-'Em. Tell the little maid to come here. (Cook *exits.*)

King Bighead. Who can this little maid be who once lived in the realm of Bighead? No one has left Bighead (*sadly*) except — (Sally *enters.*)

King Please-'Em. Ah, here is the little maid. What do you have to say for yourself?

Sally. Your Highness, I know that King Bighead likes rubies and gold.

King Please-'Em. Who doesn't?

Sally. When I baked his favorite dish, I put into it my ruby ring, set in gold.

King Please-'Em (*leans over dish*). Why here it is! A ruby ring set in gold! (*Ring shows above dish.*)

Sally. King Bighead once said that he didn't care much for salt.

King Please-'Em. Ridiculous! Everyone cares for salt. You displease me! Off with your head!

118

KING BIGHEAD. Wait! The fault is mine. It's true. I once said I didn't care for salt. Today I learned how much I love salt. Today I learned how much my daughter loves me.

KING PLEASE-'EM. I just don't understand.

KING BIGHEAD. First let me say, I am very pleased that this little maid cooked this dish for me.

KING PLEASE-'EM. You're pleased? (KING BIGHEAD *nods.*) Then, little maid, you keep your head.

SALLY. Thank you very much, your Highness.

KING BIGHEAD. King Please-'Em, I'd like to make a long story short. Don't ask me to explain. This is my daughter, Princess Sally, who has been gone from home for a long time. (*Turns to* SALLY.) Sally, will you come home with me?

SALLY. Oh, yes, Father! I'd love to go home with you. But before we leave, if King Please-'Em is willing I'd like to serve another dish of turtle-rabbit-wasps'-nest jumble, made with salt!

119

Shadow Puppets

SHADOW PUPPETS can grow large or small as they move toward the screen or away from it. They can climb a tree or mountain in an instant. They can disappear in a jiffy.

Choose a play or story in which there are only a few characters and little or no scenery. Your stage must not be crowded. Each figure must stand alone because when one figure gets behind another or behind a piece of scenery, it does not show.

The size of your puppets will depend upon the size of your stage. Cut out side-view figures from cardboard. Leave a strip 1 inch wide and 6 inches long at the base, by which to hold the puppet. Let only the figure show on the screen.

There are several kinds of shadow-puppet theaters. All of them have a frame with a piece of tissue paper or plain cotton material stretched

across the opening. The frame may be a wooden one or it may be a cardboard carton with a large hole cut in one side.

A light is placed directly behind the screen.

The operator of the puppets is below the screen and holds the puppets up between the screen and the light. The operator must stay below the path of the light and keep his hand below the stage. Experiment to see just where and how to place the light and how high to hold the puppets.

Scenery that does not change can be Scotch-taped in place behind the screen, or someone can hold it in place.

You can put on a play, speaking in a different type of voice for each puppet. Or one person can stand in front of the stage and tell a story while the operator works the puppets. If your screen is large, you can have more than one operator and more characters in your play.

To have shadow puppets in color, cut out a cardboard silhouette. Cut out the center, leaving a small frame around the edge. Glue colored cellophane or tissue paper over the opening. Light shining through the colored paper shows the color on the screen.

JIM BRIDGER AND THE WOLVES
Characters

JIM BRIDGER, scout and trapper	WOLVES, at least two
BILLY, a boy	BEAVER
SAM, another trapper	

ACT I

SCENE: *Campfire, 1850. A large pine tree is right. It may be fastened to the screen.* BILLY *sits on the ground.* JIM BRIDGER *stands near him. If the screen is large enough, there may be a campfire between them.*

BILLY. Do you think you'll get the wagon train through?

JIM. Sure 'nuff! Jim Bridger always gets his train through.

BILLY. How come you know so much about the land around here?

JIM. Used to be a trapper, son.

BILLY. A trapper? Good! Then you can answer my question. What's the smartest animal?

JIM. Why do you want to know?

121

BILLY. Tom Hall and I were arguing today. What's the smartest animal?

JIM. Depends what they're smart for. Some animals are smart for one thing. Some are smart for another.

BILLY. I don't care what it is. I just want to tell Tom something.

JIM. Well, then, I'd say the wolf.

BILLY. Why the wolf?

JIM. Why the wolf? Well, I'll take you back to long ago. Then you can figure out why I say the wolf is the smartest animal.

(Turn off lights.)

ACT II

SCENE. *The same scene, years earlier.* JIM *and* SAM *are on stage.*

SAM. Say, Jim, it's getting pretty late. Think we ought to build a fire or something?

JIM. Fire? For what?

SAM. Well, wolves, or —

JIM. Wolves? I'm not afraid of wolves.

SAM. You're not? Listen.

WOLVES *(off stage)*. *Ooowl*

JIM. Wow! They are wolves! Get up that tree! (JIM *and* SAM *climb tree. Take puppets away from screen.* WOLVES *enter.*)

WOLVES. *Ooooow!* (*Move* WOLVES *up and down when they howl.*)

SAM. Hey, Jim, I can't see you!

JIM. Let's hope the wolves can't either.

WOLVES. *Oow!*

SAM. But they can smell you.

JIM. Maybe so.

WOLVES. *Ooooow!*

SAM. Why don't you scare them away, Jim?

JIM. O.K. (*Starts singing.*) "Bury me not on the lone prairie —"

Wolves. *OOOOW!*

Sam. Your singing is worse than the howling. Look, they're going!

(Wolves *go, except one.*)

Jim. Sure enough — except one.

Sam. Sing again, Jim. Scare him too.

Jim (*singing*). "Where the coyotes howl."

Sam. Those aren't coyotes. They're wolves!

Jim (*singing*). "Where the big wolves howl and the wind blows free. Oh, bury me not (*his voice fails*) where —"

Wolf. *Oooow!*

Sam. Well, you fooled most of the wolves — all except one.

Jim. I don't think we fooled those wolves.

Sam. Why not?

Jim. They're coming back.

(Wolves *come back, bringing* Beaver.)

Sam. Sure they are. What's that animal with them?

Jim. Can't you tell? It's a beaver!

Sam. A beaver? A beaver? Oh, oh! Beavers chew down trees!

Wolves. *Oooow!*

(*Turn lights off.*)

SCENE: *Campfire, 1850.* JIM *and* BILLY *are in same positions as in* ACT I.

JIM. Now, don't you think the wolf is a smart animal? Got us up a tree. Then he got a beaver to chew down the tree.

BILLY. That wolf sure was smart, Jim. But how come you're here?

JIM. The wolf was smart, but not smart enough. He got a beaver to chew down the tree. That was smart. But a beaver likes aspen trees and Sam and I were smart enough to climb a pine tree.

(*Turn off lights.*)

Hand Puppets

HAND PUPPETS can bob up and down, nod and shake their heads, move their arms, get into fights — even pick things up in their hands.

They can be made in different ways, but their heads always have a tube inside, large enough to slip over the first finger of the operator's hand. They all wear loose dresses that can be draped over the operator's hand and wrist.

All fist puppets are worked the same way. The operator puts his first finger into the puppet's head and extends his thumb and middle finger for the puppet's arms.

If you make a fist puppet for each hand, the puppets can talk to each other, tell each other jokes and tall tales, get into arguments, or sing songs. You can also make up little plays for a number of puppets worked by several people.

Sock Fist Puppet. The head of a sock puppet is the stuffed toe of an old sock with a stiff tube inside. You can use a mailing tube, or you can make a cardboard tube a little larger than your middle finger.

Cut off the toe of the sock about 4½ inches from the end. Stuff about 3 inches of it with cotton, kapok, or old rags. Insert the tube, adjusting the stuffing to shape the head. The tube and the sock should extend a little below the stuffing. Sew a running stitch at the bottom of the stuffing. Pull the thread tight around the tube and fasten the thread.

To make features, you can sew on buttons for eyes and mouth. Or you can paint features, or cut them from cloth and sew them in place.

You can make a wig from an old sock, or you can sew on yarn hair. Or you can have a bald puppet with or without a hat. All fist puppets wear simple dresses which fit over the hand easily. An elastic at the bottom of the dress prevents it from slipping up the wrist.

ABE LINCOLN — CHAMP
Characters

Mr. Offut	Jack Armstrong	
Abe Lincoln	Eben Hall	} Clary's Grove Boys
	Bill Warren	

You can put on this play with only three puppets, having Jack *speak all the boys' lines.*

Scene. *Outside Offut's General Store.*

Mr. Offut (*comes out of store as* Boys *approach*). Howdy, boys. Come to buy something?

Jack. Naw, we came to see the giant folks say is working here.

Mr. Offut (*laughing*). Oh, you mean Abe Lincoln. Well, he sure is a big one, and smart, too — smart enough to be president.

BILL. Who care's about being smart? It's being big that counts.

OTHER BOYS. Yeah, can he fight? How good is he?

MR. OFFUT. I tell you, boys, Abe Lincoln can run faster, jump higher, throw farther, and fight better than any man in the county.

JACK. Yeah? We gotta see that. Come on, boys! (Boys *start toward store.*)

MR. OFFUT. Wait a minute, boys. Don't go in. You'll wreck the place, like you did last time. I'll call him. Abe! Abe Lincoln, come on out!

ABE (*comes out of store*). You called, Mr. Offut?

MR. OFFUT. Yes, Abe. These are the Clary's Grove boys. They want to meet you.

ABE. Howdy, boys.

EBEN (*stepping up*). So, you're the great Abe Lincoln.

ABE. That's my name. Abe Lincoln, son of Tom Lincoln.

EBEN. Old Offut's been braggin' about you.

ABE. He shouldn't have done that.

MR. OFFUT. I didn't mean anything, Abe.

EBEN. He says you can outrun anyone in the county.

ABE. Maybe so. Look at these legs. They're so long, they just start and stretch — one after the other. It's not really running.

EBEN. And outjump anybody?

ABE. Same long legs again.

EBEN. And outthrow anybody?

ABE. Well, the arms match the legs. Just born big, I guess. Glad to have met you boys. Excuse me, though. I've got work to do. (*Starts to go.*)

EBEN. Hold on! We told you we're the Clary's Grove boys.

ABE. Yes, I know.

EBEN. Mean anything to you?

ABE. I've heard tell you're quite the fighters around here. I'm a store-keeper.

127

EBEN. Old Offut says you can outfight any man in the county. When you say that to a Clary's Grove boy, you've got to prove it. There's nobody can outfight Jack Armstrong here. (*Points to* JACK.)

JACK (*stepping up*). Yeah, you didn't figure on me when you started braggin'.

MR. OFFUT (*stammering*). But — but —

ABE (*coolly*). I'm sorry, boys. I don't know why you're angry. I have no desire to fight Mr. Armstrong.

JACK (*closing in*). Mr. Armstrong, is it? Well, Mr. Lincoln, nobody calls me Mister and gets away with it. There's no sissy labels on Jack Armstrong. See? (*Gives* ABE *a punch.*)

ABE (*warding off punch*). Just a minute. If you're going to fight, I'll fight, too. (*They fight. Other boys cheer.* JACK *falls down. Other boys start to close in.*) Stand back! Sissies, I'll take you one at a time or two at a time.

JACK (*getting up*). Stand back, boys. No use fightin' Abe Lincoln. He's the best guy that ever broke into the settlement — even if he is smart enough to be president! (*Offers hand to* ABE. *They shake.*)

EBEN, BILL, and MR. OFFUT. Yeah!

SPACE UNLIMITED
Characters

JOHN   JANE

SCENE: *Inside a rocket ship. You can think of a way to change scenery, or you can imagine that the puppets are going to the moon, Mars, Jupiter, Saturn, Uranus, Neptune, and a space station.* JOHN *and* JANE *enter ship.*

JANE. Golly, John, do you think we ought to be in here?

JOHN. Sure. Why not? The airport is open for inspection. When I come to an inspection, I expect to inspect. First I am going to inspect this button.

JANE. But I saw a sign: "Keep off."

JOHN. Now listen, Jane, you don't have to come here unless you want to. The sign says: "Keep off." It doesn't say: "Keep out." I'm in and I'm going to inspect this rocket ship. First I'll inspect this button. (*Pushes button.*)

JANE. Oh, John, you closed the door!

JOHN. Well, what do you know! Wonder what this button does? (*Pushes another button. Both puppets jerk back and begin to bounce around.*)

JANE. John! John! You started the ship!

JOHN. Well, what do you know!

JANE. What'll we do?

JOHN. We're in a ship.
      We'll take a trip.
      Zip! Zip! Zip!

JANE. John, how can you? How can you sit there rhyming? Hip, hip, hip, rip, slip, tip. Oh, I'm doing it too. I'm getting dizzy. There goes New York. Pork, hork, fork —

JOHN. Say, you are getting dizzy, tizzy? No! No! You're short of oxygen. We're short of oxygen. Hey, here's an oxygenizing button.

(*Pushes button.*) That's better. Come on, Sis, enjoy the ride. Look, there's the moon!

JANE. I do feel better. Look, the moon does have mountains on it! But who'll believe us? We've seen the moon. What's happening now? I'm floating. So are you, John. (*Both puppets begin to glide around the stage.*)

JOHN. Sure enough. I'm floating and gloating.

JANE. Come on, John. I'm scared. I'm petrified.

JOHN. Oh, no, you aren't petrified. It's gravity that's petrified. Gravity's frozen — just standing still.

JANE. Well, I'm not standing still. Look, there's Mars. We've passed Mars, John.

JOHN. Passed Mars, and no one will believe us.

JANE. Look, John, Mars does have funny things on it! And canals and mountains. It's true. (*Puppets are suddenly upright.*) What did you do then?

JOHN. I pushed another button. See — gravitizer.

JANE. Gravitizer? Good! Now look for landingizer. I'd hate to stay in this ship forever.

JOHN. Well, you don't want to land here.

JANE. Golly, no! Look, that's Jupiter! See the rings — red one in the center.

JOHN. Look, there's another! Saturn, I bet. We are traveling fast. No one will believe us when we get back.

JANE. When we get back. Oh, John, how are we going to get back?

JOHN. Get back? What made you ask that? Hey look, there's a pale green something — Uranus, I bet. Jane, are you looking? How are you going to tell people what it's like if you don't look?

JANE. How are you going to tell anyone anything if you don't get back?

JOHN. Jumping Jupiter!

JANE. Jupiter doesn't jump. You and I know it doesn't jump. We saw Jupiter, but how are we going to tell people when we get back?

JOHN. Look, there's Neptune — one moon. But what's that?

JANE. John! (*Screams.*) We're heading for something. It's not a planet. It's not a star!

JOHN. Not a bird. Not a plane. Hey, what is it? We're hitting it. Push something, Jane. Push anything! We're hitting another rocket ship.

JANE. And a platform. It's a space station, John. A space station with wild-looking people on it. (*Crash off stage.*)

JOHN (*soberly*). It is a space station. And, Jane, now we're on our way to Pluto.

JANE. John, I'm tired. (*She leans back.*)

JOHN. Jane, you leaned against something. Move. (*She moves. He looks.*) Eartherizer.

JANE. This ship has everything — oxygenizer, gravitizer, and now eartherizer. John, we're going home! We touched the eartherizer!

JOHN. If we look I suppose we'll find an atomizer, insectisizer, realizer —

JANE. I found something. Rhyme this.

JOHN. What?

JANE. You have to rhyme it.

JOHN. Get out of the way. Let me see what you found!

JANE. No, sir! You have to guess. It rhymes with order.

JOHN. Border, hoarder — (JANE *moves a little*) recorder! Jane, a tape recorder!

JANE. Right you are. A tape recorder and an automatic camera.

JOHN. Yippee! Now they'll believe us. A tape recorder and an automatic camera. Ship ahoy! Space ship ahoy! (*Both puppets jump up and down.*) Oh, joy! Oh, boy! We're heading home. No more to roam. Across the foam. (*They keep rhyming as long as they can.*)

JANE and JOHN. Bump! We're home!

Rod Puppets

ROD PUPPETS, like fist puppets, are operated below the level of the stage. Each puppet stands on a pedestal. His head is attached to a dowel stick, which you can twist to make the puppet nod his head or turn it — around if you wish. His flexible arms are attached to stiff wires, which

you can move to make the puppet cross his heart, shake hands, or wave good-by.

To make a pedestal, fill a can about half full of pebbles. Mix plaster of Paris according to the directions on the package. Stand a 14½-inch dowel stick upright in the middle of the can, among the pebbles. Pour plaster mixture over the pebbles. When the plaster is hard enough to allow the stick to stand alone, set the can aside.

The head of the puppet is made separately. Fold a piece of cotton cloth in half. Draw the profile of a face with a long neck. Stitch through the two thicknesses. Cut around the stitching, leaving a narrow margin. Turn right side out. Stuff the head with cotton. Insert a 13½-inch dowel, rearranging the stuffing if necessary. Turn in the edges of the neck and glue to the dowel.

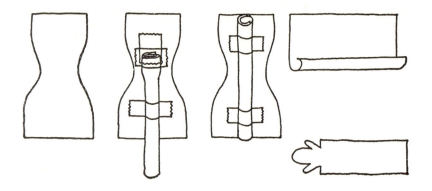

The torso, or trunk of the body, of a rod puppet has one tube down the center which holds the head dowel and one tube in front which holds the pedestal dowel.

Draw a picture of a torso on a piece of lightweight cardboard 4 inches long and 2½ inches wide. (Cracker boxes are good weight.) Cut out the body and make another just like it.

Roll a piece of lightweight cardboard 4½ inches wide and 5½ inches long into a 4½-inch tube that will fit easily over the dowel stick. Scotch-tape the overlapping edge in place, or glue it down and wind the thread around it to hold it.

Glue this tube on one cardboard torso so that the top of the tube comes to the center of the neck and extends down. Glue cotton on both sides of the tube until you have a flat surface. Glue the second torso on top of the cotton. Wind thread around the torsos to fasten together.

Make another tube from a piece of cardboard 6 inches wide and 6¼ inches long. Glue this tube on the center-front of the torso so that the top of the tube comes to the waist and extends below the torso. Put a little glue inside the top of the tube and press the top shut. Pad the torso with cotton. Wrap 2-inch strips of soft cloth around the padding. Sew the ends in place.

Make cloth arms, 5 inches long. Sew in place. Dress the puppet. Attach a 12-inch piece of heavy wire to each wrist.

134

Put the head dowel through the tube in the center of the body. Put the puppet on the pedestal dowel. Twist the center dowel to make the puppet turn his head. Push the dowel up and down a little to make him nod. Lift an arm wire to make the puppet raise his hand. To make him walk, push the pedestal can.

GRANNY'S GHOST
Characters

GRANNY	JENNY
PETER	GHOST

SCENE. *Granny's home.* GRANNY *is crying hard.* JENNY *and* PETER *are trying to comfort her.*

GRANNY. Boo, hoo, hoo!

JENNY. Why, Granny, what's the matter?

GRANNY. Boo, hoo! It's my house. It's haunted.

JENNY. Don't you like a haunted house?

GRANNY. Yes, I like a haunted house. I like my little ghost.

PETER. Then why are you crying?

GRANNY. I have to sell my house. I have to go to Florida, away from the wind and the cold. Nobody will buy a haunted house. Boo, hoo, hoo!

PETER. Now, isn't that the silliest thing you ever heard? Nobody wants to buy a haunted house!

GRANNY. It's true. Nobody wants a haunted house. Boo, hoo, hoo!

JENNY. Now, Granny, you mustn't cry. If nobody wants a haunted house, we'll have to de-haunt the house.

GRANNY. De-haunt the house! How do you de-haunt a house? I've asked the ghost to leave. It says it's lived here longer than I have. Boo, hoo, hoo!

PETER. I know. I read about a ghost town, way out West. There's nothing there now. I bet they captured the ghosts. Shot 'em through

135

the head. Strung 'em up a tree. When the ghost comes in, I'll sneak up behind it. (*Goes through motions.*) Shoot it with a toy revolver. Bang! Bang! Bang!

GRANNY. Peter! Peter! Don't hurt my little ghost. Boo, hoo, hoo!

JENNY. Come, Granny, lie down. Let Peter handle the ghost.

GRANNY. Boo, hoo, hoo! (*Exits with* JENNY.)

PETER (*looking around*). Ghost! Ghost! Wherever you are, come out and fight Peter the Great.

GHOST (*off stage*). *Owwww! Owwww!*

PETER. Hey! Where are you? (*He turns.* GHOST *enters when* PETER's *back is turned. Gets very close to him.*)

GHOST. Boo!

PETER (*jumping*). Oh!

GHOST. *Owwww! Owwww!* So you'd like to get rid of me. Listen, fellow (*advances,* PETER *backs up*), I don't aim to budge an inch. I'm here to stay.

PETER (*dodging around*). Yes, yes. I understand. You're here to stay. But I wish you would go. People don't like to buy a haunted house.

GHOST. People are very silly. Ghosts are good company — if you learn to like a ghost. *Owwww! Owwww! Owwww!* Hey! Hey! Hey!

PETER. Please go! Please go!

GHOST. Hey! Hey! Hey! You go-oo-ooo — You go-oo-ooo — (*Chases* PETER.)

PETER. All right, I'll go. (*Exits.*)

GHOST. *Owwww! Owwww!* Hey! Hey! Hey!

JENNY (*entering*). My goodness! What a racket you're making!

GHOST. Racket? Racket? Everyone has his own racket. *Owwww!*

JENNY. Well, I have a racket, too. (*Sings at top of her lungs.*) "O Sole Mio!"

GHOST. *Owwww! Owwww! Owwww!*

JENNY (*singing*). "Funiculi! Funicula! Joy is everywhere. Tra-la-la. Tra-la-la-la!"

GHOST. *Owwww! Owwww!*

JENNY. "Tra-la-la-la! Tra-la-la-la!"

(*They both continue to make a lot of noise.*)

GHOST (*weary*). Stop it! Stop it, I say! I can't stand your singing.

JENNY. I can't stand your howling. "Tra-la-la-la! Tra-la-la-la!"

GHOST. *Owwww! Owwww!*

JENNY. "Ta-ra-ra! Boom-de-ay!"

GHOST. I'm getting out of here. *OWWWW! OWWWW!* (*Exits.*)

PETER (*entering*). I'm coming back. Bang! Bang! Bang!

GRANNY (*entering*). Gracious! What's happening here?

JENNY. We got rid of the ghost, Granny. It likes to make a racket. But it doesn't like to listen to a racket.

GRANNY. Oh, poor little ghost. Boo, hoo, hoo!

PETER. Poor little ghost? I thought you wanted it to go so that you could sell the house and move to Florida.

GRANNY. So I did. Now I'll miss my little ghost. Boo, hoo, hoo!

JENNY. Granny, do stop crying.

GRANNY. Boo, hoo, hoo!

JENNY. Granny, listen. I have an idea. Ghost, come back.

GHOST (*off stage*). *Noooooo —*

JENNY. Just a minute.

GHOST (*off stage*). Noooooo —

JENNY. Half a minute.

GHOST (*entering*). Well, half a minute. I can't stand your singing any more than half a minute. *Owwww!*

JENNY (*to* GHOST). *Shhhh!* (*To* GRANNY.) Granny, why don't you take the ghost to Florida with you?

GRANNY. Ghost, will you go?

GHOST. *Owwww* —

JENNY. Will you go? (GHOST *is silent.* JENNY *sings softly.*) "Funiculi, Funicula—"

PETER. Bang! Bang!

GHOST. Yes, I'll go. Come on, Granny! Let's go! (GHOST *and* GRANNY *exit.*)

JENNY. Now the house is de-haunted. "Tra-la-la-la! Tra-la-la-la!"

PETER. Bang! Bang!

UNA FOOLS THE FIGHTING GIANT
Characters

FINN McCOUL, a giant   CUHULLIN, another giant
UNA, his wife

SCENE. *The McCoul home. On a table are several puppet-size loaves of bread.* UNA *is setting the last loaf near the others.* FINN *stands worried.*

UNA. Come, Finn McCoul! Why are you looking sad?

FINN. It's worried, I am. Plum worried.

UNA. About what people say, Finn? Let them talk. (*Imitates people talking.*) "Finn's a fool," they say. "Builds his house on a mountain. Gets wind from all directions."

FINN. Sure, it's windy up here. But I like the view.

UNA. "Sure," they say, "Finn's a fool. No water close by."

FINN. Someday I'll get water close by.

UNA. Sure, you know all the answers. Why do you worry what people say? (*Pats him on back.*)

FINN. Oh, Una, it isn't what folks say that's worrying me. It's Cuhullin.

UNA. Cuhullin, the fighting giant? Why worry about him?

FINN. Why worry about Cuhullin? When Cuhullin gets mad and stamps his foot, all Ireland shakes.

UNA. If you get mad, Finn, you can shake all Ireland, too.

FINN. Una, Cuhullin has fought every giant in the world except me. He's beaten them all. Someday he's coming to fight me. I'm worried, worried, worried! (*Puts hands up to his head.*)

UNA. Listen, Finn. I know something you don't know. And I'm not worried.

FINN. What do you know that I don't know?

UNA. Cuhullin is on his way here. I can see him.

FINN. See Cuhullin?

UNA. Sure, Finn. I can see Cuhullin. You're bigger than I am, Finn. But my eyes are better than yours. Cuhullin will be here soon.

FINN. Cuhullin be here soon? No! No! No! I'll have to fight him. I don't want to fight him! Una, what'll I do? What'll I do?

UNA. Do as I say, and you won't have to fight Cuhullin.

FINN. Una, you're dreaming. Cuhullin fights everyone. He'll fight me, too. What'll I do? Here, I'll eat some bread for strength.

UNA (*stopping him*). Stop! Don't touch those!

139

FINN (*getting worried*). Don't eat bread in my own house?

UNA (*going close to him*). *Sh!* It's a secret. (*She points to bread.*) These loaves are all right. (*She points to other loaves.*) But in the middle of these loaves are frying pans.

FINN. Frying pans? In bread? Why, Una? Why?

UNA. Never you mind why. Now do as I say. Get into bed and pretend you're a baby.

FINN. *Me?* The great Finn McCoul! Pretend I am a baby? I refuse!

UNA. All right. Then go fight Cuhullin.

FINN. I don't want to fight Cuhullin.

UNA. All right, then get into bed. Pretend you are a baby. I'll whistle for Cuhullin so he'll think he's welcome. (*Gives long, loud whistle.*)

FINN. Una, are you sure you know what you're doing? (*Exits.*)

UNA (*merrily singing*). There little baby, keep covered. Good night. Sleep tight. Wake up bright in the morning light. Do what's right with all your might. Tra-la, la-la. Oh, I do believe I have company. Come in! Come in! (CUHULLIN *enters.*) Good morning. You must be Cuhullin of whom I've heard so much. How nice of you to come all this way to pay us a call! What a pity my dear Finn is not at home! He'll be sorry to miss you.

CUHULLIN. I'll wait, ma'am. I did come a piece, and I aim to see Finn.

UNA. You came all that way, and there's only poor little me and our darling babe at home. I do wish Finn were here. You know, I think the wind is blowing on the baby. People say, "Why did Finn build his house on the mountaintop, where the wind blows so?" But you know, we like the view, and we don't mind the wind. Whenever the wind blows on the wrong side of the house, Finn turns the house around.

CUHULLIN. Turns the house around?

UNA. Yes, Finn is such a strong man! He just turns the house around when the wind blows on the baby. Would you mind turning the house around now?

CUHULLIN. Turn the house around?

UNA. Yes, Finn just lifts the house and turns it around. Can't you?

CUHULLIN. If Finn can do it, I can do it. (*Exits.*)

UNA. Tra-la, la-la —

CUHULLIN (*off stage*). *Puff, puff*! Turns the house around, does he? He's some giant to turn the house around. Well, here goes!

UNA (*twisting and nearly falling over*). Woops, little baby! I hope you like the house turned around.

FINN (*off stage*). Una, what are you doing?

UNA. Hush, little baby, hush. Here comes Cuhullin. (*Enter* CUHULLIN.) Thank you, Cuhullin. You are very kind. You turn the house around just the way that Finn turns it when the wind blows in the wrong direction.

CUHULLIN. *Hmmmm.*

UNA. Now I know you must be thirsty. (*Looks to side.*) Oh, dear! The water bucket is empty, and a big rock fell on the spring after Finn left. Whenever that happens, Finn lifts a new rock for me to find a spring underneath. Will you go out and lift that rock for me? (*She points outside.*)

CUHULLIN (*looks in direction* UNA *points*). Lift that rock? It's a cliff! One side of a mountain!

141

UNA. I know. But it is just the kind of rock that Finn lifts when he is looking for water. Well, maybe it is too big for you.

CUHULLIN. If Finn can lift it, I can lift it. (*Exits.*)

UNA. Tra-la, la-la — Hope you like the new spring, little baby.

CUHULLIN (*off stage*). *Puff, puff, puff!* If Finn can lift this rock, I can lift it. *Puff!* There! (*Enters.*)

UNA. Oh, thank you, kind Cuhullin. You lift rocks just the way that my Finn lifts rocks. Now I know you are ready to eat. Here, take a loaf of bread. (*She hands him one of the loaves in which there is a frying pan. He takes one bite.*)

CUHULLIN (*in pain*). Hey! Hey! What's the matter? My tooth! My teeth!

UNA. What's wrong?

CUHULLIN. What's wrong? What's right? Your bread's so hard I broke my tooth on it. I mean my teeth. Ohhhh!

UNA. I can't understand it. Even Little Finn, our baby, loves my bread. Here, I'll give him a loaf. (*Takes a loaf without frying pan in it and goes off stage.*)

CUHULLIN. My tooth! My teeth! I'll never be the same! How miserable I am!

FINN (*dressed like baby enters eating bread and talking baby talk*). Hello. Don't you like my mamma's bread? I think it's wonderful.

CUHULLIN. You eat that bread? Who are you?

FINN. I'm Little Finn. My daddy likes my mamma's bread. Don't you?

CUHULLIN. Little Finn? You're a big boy.

FINN. Someday I'll be as big as my daddy.

CUHULLIN. Wow! How big is your daddy?

FINN. Oh, he's very big—bigger than this room. He bends down when he comes in. Want another piece of bread?

CUHULLIN. No, thank you! Your daddy's bigger than this room?

FINN (*nodding*). Mm-hmmmm.

CUHULLIN. He likes that bread?

FINN (*nodding*). Sure does.

CUHULLIN. He pulls up mountains when he wants water?

FINN (*nodding*). Mm-hmmmm.

CUHULLIN. He turns the house around when the wind blows in the wrong direction?

FINN. Yes, he does.

CUHULLIN (*coming close*). Say, does he like to fight?

FINN (*backing away*). Fight? Nobody wants to fight my daddy. He's too big.

CUHULLIN. Well, I don't want to fight your daddy either. Good-by! (*Exits.*)

FINN. Good-by! Come back when Mamma bakes bread again. (*He waves until he is sure* CUHULLIN *is out of sight. Then he laughs and laughs.*)

UNA (*entering*). Good-by, Cuhullin. Come back when we need a new spring or when we need the house turned around again. Ha, ha, ha!

FINN (*hugging* UNA). Oh, Una, I don't have to fight Cuhullin!

UNA. No, Finn, now you'll never have to fight Cuhullin.

Marionettes

A MARIONETTE is a puppet operated by strings. He can jump, dance, sit down, bow, wave his hands — even fly. You can buy marionettes, or you can make simple ones yourself. The body may be a loose-jointed rag doll. Or you can make a marionette with papier-mâché head, lath shoulders and hips, and tape body, legs, and arms. Be sure to sew weights in the feet and hands.

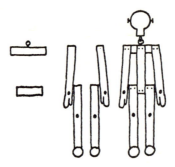

You operate a marionette with a control bar which has strings attached. The main control has strings extending from the front to the marionette's wrists. Another string extends from the back of the bar to the marionette's seat.

A shorter bar is nailed across the main bar. Strings extend from this to the sides of the marionette's head.

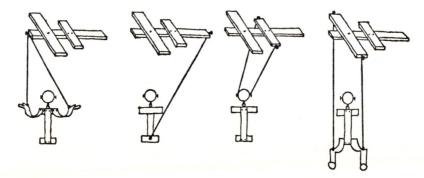

A third bar is removable. It may fit on a peg or nail on the main bar. Strings extend from it to the knees of the marionette.

You can make animals or queer-creature marionettes from small boxes, scraps of wood, pipestem cleaners, and other odds and ends. Attach strings to them.

To operate a marionette, hold the main control bar in your left hand so that the marionette's feet touch the floor or a table. Pull the front

strings with your right hand to make the marionette's arms move. Sing a song, having the marionette's arm move in rhythm.

Pull the strings from the small crossbar to make the marionette turn his head. Tilt the bar and lift the back string to make him bow. Say a few lines, having the marionette move in a natural way.

To make him walk, continue to hold the main control in your left hand. Remove the front bar with your right. Pull the strings. Twist the bar. See the different movements he makes.

When you have learned to operate your marionette, have him perform to music. If a friend has a marionette, the two of you might sing ballads which have questions and answers and refrains, like "The

Keeper," which has the refrain: "Jacky-boy!" "Master!" "Sing ye well?" "Very well," etc.

If two or three friends are ready to put on a play, use a recorded story with the marionettes acting, as the narrator tells the tale. Then put on a simple play, speaking the lines and also operating the marionette. Learn your lines! Don't try to operate a marionette and read backstage at the same time.

As your interest in marionettes grows, work on harder plays. Construct a theater. Construct a troop of marionettes for you and your friends to operate. There is no limit to the wonderful things that you can do with marionettes.

HASTE AWAY TO THE WEDDING

This ballad is sung to the tune of "The Bear Went Over the Mountain." One puppet is JENNY; *the other,* JOHNNY.

JENNY and JOHNNY (*together*).
> Haste away to the wedding.
> Haste away to the wedding.
> Haste away to the wedding,
> Jenny (Johnny), my own true love.

JENNY.
> What'll I wear to the wedding?
> What'll I wear to the wedding?
> What'll I wear to the wedding,
> Johnny, my own true love?

JOHNNY.
> Your old clothes, to be sure.
> Your old clothes, to be sure.
> Your old clothes, to be sure,
> Jenny, my own true love.

146

(*Following verses have these first lines.*)
JENNY. How shall we go to the wedding?
JOHNNY. We'll walk down to the church.

JENNY. What shall we eat at the wedding?
JOHNNY. Black bread and bean soup.

JENNY. Where shall we live when we're married?
JOHNNY. In that shed back of the barn.

JENNY. How much do you love me, Johnny?
JOHNNY. I never thought of it, Jenny.

JENNY. Then find another bride.
JOHNNY (*speaks*). Wait a minute! I do love you, Jenny, very much.
You'll have — (*sings*)
      A new dress when we're married;
      Good food when we're married;
      A new house when we're married,
      Jenny, my own true love.

JENNY and JOHNNY (*come close together and sing*).
　　Then haste away to the wedding.
　　Haste away to the wedding.
　　Haste away to the wedding,
　　Jenny (Johnny), my own true love.

OWWWWW — OWWWWW!

Everyone takes part in this poem stunt. You read the poem, the audience joins in the refrain, operators help creature marionettes to act out the verses.

　　When odd little creatures go out at night,
　　They fill us all with scary fright.
REFRAIN. *Owwwww — Owwwww!*

　　They wiggle and writhe. They jump and hop.
　　They pounce up high and land *ker-plop!*
REFRAIN. *Owwwww — Owwwww!*

　　Now over them reigns a queer man from Mars,
　　A horrible creature, marked with scars.
REFRAIN. *Owwwww — Owwwww!*

148

When he throws up his arms and shakes his head,
All earthly beings are filled with dread.
REFRAIN. *Owwwww — Owwwww!*

The creatures draw close with no fear or fright.
He whispers, "Now who'll we scare tonight?"
REFRAIN. *Owwwww — Owwwww!*

With fury they yell, "We'll tell you true!
The ones we'll scare are *you* and *you*." (*Narrator points to
two people in the audience.*)
REFRAIN. *Owwwww — Owwwww!* (*Very loud.*)

THE FAIRY IN THE DELL
Characters

KATHLEEN   GIANT
FAIRY

SCENE: *A wooded dell.* KATHLEEN *is alone, singing.*

KATHLEEN. The fairy in the dell;
                The fairy in the dell;
                Hi! Ho! The merry, oh!
                The fairy in the dell.
FAIRY (*entering*). Did you call me?

KATHLEEN. I don't think so. Who are you?

FAIRY. I'm the fairy in the dell. Didn't I hear you singing "The fairy in the dell"?

KATHLEEN. You surely did. But I wasn't singing about you. (FAIRY *hangs her head.*) Oh, please, don't look so sad. I couldn't sing about you because I didn't know that you existed.

FAIRY. Then why did you sing "The fairy in the dell"?

KATHLEEN. I'll tell you, but it may sound silly.

FAIRY. Oh, no, it won't. Nothing sounds silly to fairies.

KATHLEEN. Well, every day we sing "The Farmer in the Dell. The Farmer in the Dell." I get tired of it. I get tired of hearing about the farmer, and I get tired of being the farmer, the dog, or the cheese. So I thought, Why not sing "The fairy in the dell"?

FAIRY. Why did you come here to sing "The fairy in the dell"?

KATHLEEN. I don't want to hurt your feelings. But I'll tell you if you really want to know.

FAIRY. Please do.

KATHLEEN. Well, most of the children don't believe in fairies. I didn't want to have them laugh at me, so I came out here to sing alone. Now I don't have to sing alone, because you can sing with me.

FAIRY. Fine! I'd like to sing.

FAIRY and KATHLEEN (*singing*).

> The fairy in the dell;
> The fairy in the dell;
> Hi! Ho! The merry, oh!
> The fairy in the dell.

(*Loud crash, off stage.*)

GIANT (*off stage*). Grrrr!

KATHLEEN. Oh, dear! What's that?

FAIRY. That's the horrible Giant of the dell.

KATHLEEN. I've got to get out of here.

FAIRY. You can't.

150

KATHLEEN. I can't? Why not?

FAIRY. The Giant has trapped you. You can't escape by your legs. You just might escape by your wits. No one ever has, but you might. Boo, hoo, hoo! Why did I let you sing? Why didn't I tell you?

KATHLEEN. For goodness' sakes, tell me now! How can I escape by my wits? Tell me before the Giant gets here.

FAIRY. He's still a long way off. Listen. The Giant has cast a spell

on this dell. He hates fairies because he is big, and yet he cannot crush a fairy. So if a human comes here and mentions a fairy, the Giant captures the human and will not let him go unless he can answer three riddles.

KATHLEEN. Do you know the riddles?

FAIRY. Yes, I know the riddles. They are old-fashioned riddles with old-fashioned answers. I know two answers. You will have to figure out the third.

KATHLEEN. Tell me! Quickly!

FAIRY. The first riddle is: What is whiter than new-fallen snow?

KATHLEEN. And the answer?

FAIRY. A soul without sin.

KATHLEEN. A soul without sin?

FAIRY. Yes, a soul without sin. Someday you'll know the meaning. Just remember the answer now.

KATHLEEN. The second?

FAIRY. What is blacker than the blackest night?

KATHLEEN. The answer?

FAIRY. An ungrateful heart.

GIANT (*off stage*). *Grrrr!*

FAIRY. He's almost here. Good luck! (FAIRY *disappears.*)

KATHLEEN (*crying*). Fairy, Fairy, where are you? Where are you? What's the last question? What shall I do? What will my mother say if I don't come home? What was the first question? What was the second? Oh, here comes the Giant! I'll pretend I'm not afraid.

(GIANT *enters.*)

KATHLEEN. Good afternoon, sir. It's a very nice day.

GIANT. Oh, yes, a nice day to eat a little girl like you.

KATHLEEN. Oh, no, sir. You must be mistaken.

GIANT. Mistaken? What makes you think I am mistaken?

KATHLEEN. I know you are mistaken. If this were a nice day to eat little girls, my mother would have told me.

GIANT. Your mother would have told you?

KATHLEEN. Yes, my mother always says, "Now this is a nice day to air the bedding." Or "This is a nice day to wash windows." Or "This is a nice day to play outdoors." Never, never has she said, "This is a nice day to eat little girls."

GIANT. Ho! Ho! Ho! If your mother has told you so much, maybe she has told you the answers to my riddles. Do you know what a riddle is?

KATHLEEN. Oh, yes, a riddle is a question with an answer that makes you think.

GIANT. All right, then. I'll give you three riddles. If you get the answers right, I'll let you go. If you guess wrong, I'll eat you up. The first riddle: What is whiter than new-fallen snow?

KATHLEEN. I know. I know. A soul without sin.

GIANT (*jumping up and down*). Curses! Well, try this one. What is blacker than the blackest night?

KATHLEEN. I know. An ungrateful heart.

GIANT. Curses again! Are you ready for the third question?

KATHLEEN. Oh, please, sir, won't you let me go with two riddles? Think how upset my mother will be if I don't get home by dark. Please, I'll never come to your dell again if you let me go.

GIANT. Then I'll eat you now without asking the third riddle.

KATHLEEN (*getting angry*). No, sir! That's not the bargain! I'll answer your riddle and then *you* can't come to the dell again.

GIANT. All right. If you can answer my riddle, I'll never come to the dell again. What is brighter than the stars at night?

KATHLEEN (*thinking*). What is brighter than the stars at night?

GIANT. Ha, ha, ha! Yes, what is brighter than the stars at night? Try to answer that. Ha, ha, ha!

KATHLEEN. I know! I know! I know!

GIANT. Then tell me. Tell me! What is brighter than the stars at night?

KATHLEEN. My mother's eyes are brighter than the stars at night.

GIANT. Curses! Ten times curses! A mother's eyes. Yes, that's the answer. *Grrrrrrr.* (*He disappears.*)

KATHLEEN. He's gone. He's gone! The Giant's gone! Fairy, Fairy! The Giant's gone!

FAIRY (*reappearing*). Yes, the Giant's gone, forever and **ever.**
KATHLEEN. Really? Forever and ever?
FAIRY. Yes, really. Forever and ever. Let's sing again!
KATHLEEN. Yes, let's. I know a new verse.

A mother's eyes are bright;
Bright as the stars at night.

FAIRY (*joining in*).   Hi! Ho! The merry, oh!

A mother's eyes are bright.

FAIRY. I know another. The Giant's left the dell.
KATHLEEN (*joining in*). The Giant's left the dell.

Hi! Ho! The merry, oh!
The Giant's left the dell.

Index

155

More to Read

As your interest in dramatics grows, you may want to learn more about acting, costuming, stagecraft, and puppetry. You may want to find more plays. Here is a list of books which may help you.

Acting and Costuming

Costume Book for Parties and Plays, by Joseph Leeming (Lippincott)
Costuming a Play, by Elizabeth Berkeley Grimball and Rhea Wells (Appleton)
Do It Yourself! Tricks, Stunts, and Skits, by Bernice Wells Carlson (Abingdon)
First Book of Stage Costume and Make-Up, by Barbara Berk (Watts)

Plays

Caddie Woodlawn: A Play, by Carol Ryrie Brink (Macmillan)
New Plays for Red Letter Days, by Elizabeth Hough Sechrist and Janette Woolsey (Macrae Smith)
100 Plays for Children, ed. by A. S. Burack (Plays, Inc.)
Radio Plays for Children, by Katherine Williams Watson (Wilson)
Special Plays for Special Days, by Mildred Hark and Noel McQueen (Plays, Inc.)
Stories to Dramatize, by Winifred Ward (Children's Theatre Press)

Puppets

Easy Puppets, by Gertrude Jaeckel Pels (Crowell)
First Book of Puppets, by Moritz Jagendorf (Watts)

Fun for One — or Two, by Bernice Wells Carlson (Abingdon)

Fun-Time Puppets, by Carrie Rasmussen (Children's Press)

Handbook of Fist Puppets, by Bessie A. Ficklen (Lippincott)

Let's Make a Puppet, by Blanche Wheeler and Helen Farnam (Webb)

Make It Yourself! Handicraft for Boys and Girls, by Bernice Wells Carlson (Abingdon)

Marionettes; Easy to Make! Fun to Use! by Edith Flack Ackley (Lippincott)

Penny Puppets, Penny Theatre, and Penny Plays, by Moritz Jagendorf (Bobbs-Merrill)

Puppet Book, by Helen Jill Fletcher and Jack Deckter (Greenberg)

Puppets and Marionettes, by Roger Lewis (Knopf)

Remo Bufano's Book of Puppetry (Macmillan)